Wooden Chairs
for the
Home

Anthony Hontoir

The Crowood Press

First published in 2002 by
The Crowood Press Ltd
Ramsbury, Marlborough
Wiltshire SN8 2HR

British Library Cataloguing-in-Publication Data
A catalogue record for this book is available from the British Library.

ISBN 1 86126 237 X

Typeset by Textype, Cambridge
Printed and bound in Singapore by Craft Print International Ltd.

Contents

CHAPTER 1

Something to Sit On

Chairs hardly existed before the Middle Ages, and even then they were comparatively rare. In those days, only important people would have been entitled to occupy anything so exalted as a chair; the rest of the population would have had to make do with stools and benches. All furniture was confined to necessities, and few people had time to relax in comfort. Early designs were heavily, and unsurprisingly, influenced by the church, as were so many other aspects of daily life at that time, but the gradual evolutionary process has relegated everything to its proper place in history, and now we are able to pick and choose designs according to our own personal tastes and whims, with historical detail merely providing a background to guide our likes and desires.

Certainly there is much to learn from the past, whilst at the same time there is no shortage of new ideas to explore in the future. When we set out to make wooden chairs for the home, most of our efforts are based on an amalgamation of styles, ancient and modern. It is not by chance that there is a Gothic expression amongst the contents of this book – somehow, in spite of it being from the earliest days of chair-making, it has a curiously timeless quality. Nowadays, there is a reason to put a chair in every room of the house, and today's household also includes the conservatory and the garden.

Chairs have undergone many changes over the years and, if you think about it, they have so much in common with the individual – they are basically the same, but always different.

There have been periods of grand elegance and periods of gross utility; there have been exuberance and modesty, beauty and plainness, even, if you will, the practical and the impractical. So, does a chair have a personality of its own more than any other piece of furniture? Perhaps this is a debatable question, but it is a fact that the chair develops a close association with the individual who occupies rather than uses it. We have all heard it said that 'this is so-and-so's chair', rather as if it has become an extension of the person.

If the earliest chairs were hard and uncomfortable, mere platforms for the posterior composed of unyielding planks, it is not always the case that our present liking for comfort has supplanted the solid wooden seat with luxurious upholstery. The wooden chair commands attention in all its forms, and perhaps it always will. If anything has happened to increase the potential for greatness in this piece of furniture, it has been the discovery of different woods from other parts of the world, and the artistry that has been applied by chair-makers to the craft of producing this most basic of necessities.

Not surprisingly, mass production has led to an over-simplification of the chair in many ways, namely the pressure to produce large quantities at low cost, and the unintended practice of rendering a classical design destitute through superabundance. Perhaps that explains why people are increasingly inclined to turn away from the commercially made offerings and wonder instead what they can make for themselves. We are surrounded by a wealth of ideas, so all we have to do is put them into action.

This book will help to get you started, but it should do more than provide you with a selection of plans and instructions. It should also encourage you to think about chairs in general, the purpose for which you wish to build one, how you make the best choice of material, the most appropriate type of finish, whether it needs to be upholstered and, if so, how to choose a fabric that is compatible with the design of the chair.

There may occasionally be a temptation to modify the design to produce a chair more to your own particular liking, but before you do so, it would be wise to consider if any alteration would compromise the stability or safety of the chair. If, for example, a chair were to be made bigger, it is only reasonable to assume that at some time in its life, it might have to accommodate a large heavy person, so do the joints need to be strengthened, or the seat rails enlarged, together with the seat itself? Conversely, if you wanted to make a chair smaller, to suit a child perhaps, to what extent can you reduce the material dimensions and the joint sizes before it becomes unsafe? The answers to these questions have much to do with the theory of chair design and the recognized properties of wood in all its differing varieties; it is not the scope of this book to deal with such matters.

We all have our own ideas of what constitutes good taste and what is most appealing to the eye. As with all objects that form part of our daily lives, something that strongly attracts one individual may put off another; and I must confess that whilst I admire certain modern designs and find them interesting, I am usually drawn more towards the style that could best be described as reproduction. The best of it is a simple expression of elegance, and as the chairs progress through the book, commencing with the simplest and ending with the most difficult, the final chapter is devoted to the making of a chair that dates from the late-eighteenth century, a mahogany Chippendale in its original true form, a chair of wonderful simplicity and proportion.

One of the principal aims of this book is that none of the chairs should be unduly hard to build, and that anyone with a modicum of woodworking ability should be able to produce good results without having to possess a fully equipped workshop with a large number of expensive and complicated tools. In fact, everything that is described in the following pages could easily be achieved with a modest outlay of basic handtools. Electric tools are often desirable, but they are certainly not essential although, as you will see, some are more important than others, and I would prefer not to be without them myself.

Nothing now remains except to wish you good luck with your chair-making, in the hope that it gives you much enjoyment and plenty of usefulness for many years to come.

CHAPTER 2

Materials and Tools

Before you can begin making a piece of furniture, whether it is a chair or anything else, you must decide what sort of wood you are going to use. For instance, you need to think about the appearance of the finished article, its texture, its durability, and there is the important matter of obtaining it in the right quantity and for an acceptable price. If you are making a particular type of chair, its design may imply the use of one variety of wood, for reasons that will become apparent throughout the book.

The fact that most of us live reasonably near to a timber yard may not, in itself, be much help. The vast majority of the timber stocked by these merchants falls into the category known as softwood, used extensively in carpentry and joinery, whereas much fine furniture-making, including chairs, uses hardwood. The terms 'softwood' and 'hardwood' can be misleading, for the names suggest that hardwoods are tough and durable, whilst softwoods are weaker and more susceptible to breakage. In fact, certain hardwoods are relatively soft, and a few of the softwoods are particularly hard, so clearly the generic name is misleading, for it does not refer to the actual hardness or softness of the material.

There is another reason for establishing the classification. In the colder regions of the world, such as Scandinavia, Canada and Russia, are the huge forests of evergreen coniferous trees that bear needles and cones. These provide us with softwood. In the tropical regions of Africa, Central and South America, and parts of Indonesia where, in recent years, there have

been widespread acts of deforestation, you will find only deciduous trees that shed their leaves each year. These are the hardwood trees. In other parts of the world, including most of Europe, where the climate is, by comparison, far more temperate, the trees are a mixture of the two. There are a few notable exceptions to this classification. The holly tree, for example, is classed as a hardwood, yet it keeps its leaves all year.

The difference between softwood and hardwood is not restricted to the simple matter of whether the tree loses its leaves or not as a regular annual event, the structure of the wood is also quite different. As a rule, softwood trees grow quite rapidly and have larger distances between their growth rings than hardwoods, though this is not always the case. Hardwoods,

The British countryside is home to many deciduous trees – this fine sycamore is one example.

on the other hand, generally have a finer grain structure compared with the coarser softwoods, and the texture is usually more refined. Such qualities will only become apparent when you work with many different woods, and learn to appreciate how one type varies from another in its feel, the way it cuts and in its often distinctive smell. Western red cedar, for example, has a strong aromatic odour, totally different from oak or mahogany.

Most of the wood used in chair-making is traditionally of the hardwood variety as this sort possesses the qualities considered most desirable for this kind of work. It would, however, be completely wrong to assume that hardwood is the only acceptable material for this purpose, since we would be denying the popularity of pine, which has the advantage of being considerably cheaper to buy.

In fact, pine furniture in general has become widely accepted, and is very likely to be found in the kitchen and bedroom, although hardwood retains its lead in versatility and quality since, by virtue of it being a general heading, it embraces such a wide range of woods. Of course, in recent years, chair-makers have pushed the boundaries further than ever, to include composite materials such as plywood, and methods of construction such as laminating, and these have contributed to an ever-increasing diversity in design.

As far as this book is concerned, the chairs discussed reflect some sort of balance between the imaginative and the traditional, with a little bit of a mix between the two, and this is reflected in the choice of material, so that the majority use hardwood of one sort or another and a minority are made of softwood or, more particularly, pine. Plywood has its own small contribution to make and, in reality, the reader can decide whether to opt for hardwood or softwood, as in the case of the pine dining-chair, which would look just as good, if not better, in oak.

A great deal depends on what sort of wood you already have in stock, or how easily you can get hold of it. It is an intriguing thought, but if you have amassed a sizeable collection of off-cuts over the years from other types of woodwork, and your woodpile consists of many different woods, there is nothing to stop you making this a feature of your chair; using more than one variety of hardwood, the equivalent of a patchwork quilt, if done with care, could result in a chair that could be a unique masterpiece. After all, you do not always have to follow convention.

The acquisition of wood offers a few possibilities, and it is a good idea to approach the subject with an open mind.

The Timber Merchant   Arriving at the wood-yard, the first thing you notice is that all the timber is stacked high in large, open sheds. Many timber merchants are inevitably limited in the range of woods they stock, but you can usually order some of the less well-known types and get them cut to your required sizes. Wood may be purchased in one of two forms; sawn or planed. When cut from the log, and subsequently sawn into smaller sections, the surface of the wood is rather coarse, and as such is usually only suited to work that remains out of sight. Apart from this, the main characteristic of sawn wood is with regard to its dimensions, for if a particular piece is quoted as being 50 × 25mm (2 × 1in) in cross-section, that is exactly what it should measure.

Planed wood is also known by the initials PSE (planed square edge) or PAR (planed all round). In contrast to sawn wood, it has its sides and edges prepared from the roughly sawn state by passing it through a planing machine, which skims off some of the surface to leave a smooth finish. To obtain this result, there must clearly be some reduction in the dimensions of the material, equal to the amount taken off by the plane. Prepared wood is therefore fractionally smaller in cross-section than its sawn equivalent, and there are two ways in which it may be quoted. For example, the same 50 × 25mm (2 × 1in) piece in the planed form can be referred to either as 50 × 25mm (2 × 1in) prepared, or 47 × 22mm (1⅞ × ⅞in) in the grain. Another African hardwood in the same family is utile. Between them, sapele and utile serve the chair-maker well, providing an excellent substitute for mahogany. They are both hard, easy to work, and produce a fine quality finish.

Walnut Much of the furniture built during the eighteenth century was made from this wood. It is golden brown in colour, fairly hard, close-grained, and has scarcely any tendency to warp or shrink, except in the form of satin walnut. A darker version is American black walnut.

There are, of course, many other woods – some equally well-known, others far more obscure – and it is one of the chief pleasures of woodwork to explore new materials. As your knowledge and experience of chair-making increase, the task of selecting the best wood becomes a matter of instinct.

TOOLS

Whether you are a newcomer to woodwork, with only a small set of tools, or an experienced practitioner with an extensive tool-kit, it is one of the main aims of this book to show you how to build a variety of attractive and practical chairs without the need for a vast array of complex and costly tools. For those who possess a well-equipped workshop full of power-tools, it obviously makes sense to put these to full use, but you should not be under the impression that you cannot achieve good results without them. Hand-tools may take longer, and require greater dexterity in their use, but they are in no way inferior.

There are, naturally, a number of tools that must be regarded as absolutely essential if you are to produce top-quality results. Some of these might appear at first sight to duplicate the function of others, but they all have their own special purpose and it is usually a mistake to attempt an action for which the tool was not intended. Let us consider the types of tool that you should aim to include in your tool cabinet.

Tape Measure All furniture-making depends for its success on accurate measurement, and the rule or tape is probably used more than any other single tool. My own choice is the spring-loaded flexible steel tape-measure which pulls out from a metal casing, has a lock to hold it in any position, and retracts back into the casing when not in use. The scale is marked on one face in inches and centimetres. An L-shaped steel lip is attached to the free end of the tape, and serves to mark the zero position. When the tape is calibrated in imperial and metric measurements, always take care not to mix them up. For example, it is never a good idea to start working in inches and then convert to millimetres in the middle of a project, as there will always be a slight difference in the conversion process, and in high-class furniture-making there is no room for error. Despite the onward march of metrication, many people still prefer to work in inches.

The Pencil You might think that there are already enough pencils lying around the house without having to buy one especially for woodwork. I normally use an ordinary HB pencil, which I keep well-sharpened to retain a fine point. Do not use a pencil with a hard lead, because this will score the surface of the wood. Neither do you want a very soft lead, since this quickly loses its fine point. An HB lead is a good compromise.

A retractable steel tape measure.

The Marking Knife This is used to mark a thin line on the surface of the wood, as in the case of going over the previously-squared pencil line of a tenon, so that the teeth of the saw, when cutting on the waste side of the line, do not rip up the grain beyond the line and disfigure the wood.

The Square When marking wood, it is the usual practice to draw a line at right-angles to its length. The square consists of a rectangular wooden handle, edged in brass, which has a steel blade attached to it at 90 degrees with two parallel edges. A somewhat more sophisticated version of the plain try-square is the mitre square, whose adjustable blade can be set at any angle between 45 degrees and 90 degrees.

The Mortise Gauge This tool is used to scribe two parallel lines along a piece of wood, as with the marking out of a mortise and tenon joint, and it has two spurs, one of which is fixed, the other adjustable, so that the gap between the two parallel lines may be set as required. The best types of mortise gauge are equipped with a rounded brass thumbscrew at the opposite end from the spurs, to control the position of the inner moveable spur with great precision. The sliding wooden fence, which is released and tightened by means of a screw, can be locked in any position. Most mortise gauges

combine two functions by having the double spurs for the marking of mortises and suchlike, but when needed, the adjustable spur can be tucked into the fence to leave only the fixed spur for single line marking.

The Tenon Saw As its name implies, the tenon saw is used for cutting tenons and other types of joint. It is quite a short saw, and has between twelve and twenty teeth to the inch. The top edge of the blade is strengthened with a steel or brass back to give rigidity and ensure a straight cut, and for that reason it is also known as the backsaw. The blade length ranges from 200mm (8in) to 305mm (12in). A firm wooden handgrip is an advantage.

The Handsaw This is a general-purpose saw, which you will use to do most of your preparatory cutting. It normally measures around 610mm (24in) in length, and has either eight or ten teeth to the inch. The teeth are set in an alternating pattern, so that as the saw cuts into the wood it creates a passage known as the kerf, which is wider than the thickness of the blade, thus ensuring that it does not bind or jam. The handsaw does not have a strengthened back, so it is flexible, and the manipulation of this type of saw requires some skill to maintain a perfectly straight cut.

The mortise gauge, which can also serve as a marking gauge.

A wide-bladed bevelled chisel.

The Coping Saw A very useful saw when you need to cut curves. The thin blade is mounted in a metal frame shaped in the form of a U, and held under tension by tightening the handgrip. If the handgrip is slackened off, the blade can be rotated about its axis within the frame to set it at any desired angle.

The Electric Jigsaw In its most common form, this is a hand-held power tool in which the saw blade oscillates up and down at very high speed to provide a fast and highly manoeuvrable means of cutting. Various blades may be fitted, ranging from fine to coarse.

The Chisel It is advisable to have a set of chisels covering a range of sizes so that you can select the most suitable width of blade for the job in hand. Typical blade widths would be 6mm (¼in), 9mm (⅜in), 13mm (½in), 16mm (⅝in), 19mm (¾in) and 25mm (1in). The firmer chisel has a strong cutting blade with square edges, whereas the bevelled chisel has two sloped edges, making the tool ideal for cutting dovetail joints, although dovetails do not appear in any of the projects in this book.

The Smoothing Plane This is the most frequently used bench plane. It is made from steel, and is fitted with either a wooden or plastic handle and knob. The cutter blade is easily detachable for sharpening and, when installed against the backiron, is provided with a lateral adjustment lever.

The Electric Plane This is a high-speed tool that does much the same work as the smoothing plane, except that the physical effort is reduced and the task of planing down the wood made a lot quicker. The planing action is facilitated by a revolving drum which carries two identical blades placed 180 degrees apart. As the drum, spins at speeds of up to 20,000 rpm, the blades alternately come into contact with the surface of the wood and remove small amounts as the plane is pushed forward. There is a knob for altering the depth, which works by raising or lowering the sole at the front, whilst the position of the spinning drum remains constant. With prolonged use, the rubber drive belt has a tendency to snap, and occasionally needs replacing with a new one, but this is an easy task.

The Spokeshave The function of the spokeshave is mainly to shape curved surfaces, and it is an invaluable tool for shaping the curved legs of chairs. It may not be called into

The smoothing plane.

use often, but it is an excellent tool when required.

The Handbrace This tool is used for the majority of drilling operations. It consists of a crank forged from steel, which is fitted with a rounded wooden or plastic handle at one end and a chuck at the other, for holding a variety of drill bits. When choosing a brace, opt for one that has a ratchet movement because this is invaluable when working in tight corners.

The Pillar Drill This is a very useful piece of equipment in the workshop, for it permits you to drill holes with great precision. The drill is powered by an electric motor, and may have a

The pillar drill – a very useful tool for any workshop.

variety of speeds, and the drilling action is controlled by a spring-loaded up-and-down movement. This machine is excellent for drilling out the first stage of waste from mortises.

The Electric Router There is always an element of mystery about a tool which has a reputation for performing many functions, such as rebating, grooving, fluting and edge-moulding, but in fact the electric router is simply a motor housed vertically inside the body of the tool, which drives a chuck at very high revolutions. Into the chuck may be fitted a wide range of cutters. These include straight cutters for making rebates, housing grooves and mortises; semi-circular cutters for fluting; and Roman ogee and corner round cutters for working edge-moulding patterns. The base of the router is circular, so that it can be lined up beside a length of straight-edged batten, acting as a guide, and steered through any angle without deviating from a straight path. A detachable fence can be mounted beneath the base to provide the router with its own adjustable guide, and the spring-loaded plunging action of the body may be pre-set against a scaled depth stop so that the cutter is accurately controlled both laterally and vertically.

The Lathe If you possess your own lathe, your workshop is very well equipped indeed! For occasional wood-turning, it is hardly worth investing a lot of money in a full-sized model, but you can purchase miniature lathes and attachments powered by electric drills, from which surprisingly good results can be obtained.

CARING FOR TOOLS

The most effective way of looking after all your woodworking tools is to store them away safely when not in use. If your workplace is in the garage or garden shed, where the atmosphere is likely to be damp, you can safeguard all steel

The lathe attachment is a rudimentary device, powered by an electric drill, but gives scope to produce reasonable results in wood-turning.

surfaces from rust by giving them a regular rub over with a soft cloth soaked in light oil.

Inspect saw blades, chisels and planes regularly to ensure that their cutting edges are always keen and efficient. An oilstone is an absolute must for periodically re-sharpening chisels and planes.

Remember, also, that many tools are designed to cut wood, and they are none too particular about cutting careless fingers as well. Learn how to hold and manipulate these tools properly, and stay safe at all times.

CHAPTER 3

Jointing Techniques

Successful woodworking in general, and chair-making in particular, depends on the ability to cut accurate joints. None of the jointing methods used in this book is especially complicated, but each one requires a certain amount of practice and experience in order to obtain the best results, so it is only reasonable to expect that a woodworker with a thorough knowledge of joints, and many years' practical application of that knowledge, will be in a stronger position to produce first-class work than a complete novice.

And yet, if the aspiring chair-maker is determined to apply considerable care and patience to the task, there is no reason why the beginner should not achieve an excellent standard of craftsmanship. Experience helps, but a willingness to learn is often the way to get good results.

There are a great many joints used in woodwork generally, but these can be narrowed down to a much smaller number, which are relevant to the making of chairs. Although it is not the purpose of this book to instruct the reader in the minute technical details of joint-making, it will, nonetheless, be a useful exercise to go through each of the most common and significant types of joint that appear in these pages.

THE BUTT JOINT

A butt joint is formed when the squared and planed edges or sides of two pieces of wood are brought together, or the edge of one piece and the side of the other. Although the butt joint is the simplest means of effecting a join between two pieces of wood, this most basic of joints has the ability to turn up in various shapes and sizes according to circumstances.

The main point in its favour is the ease with which it can be made. Being a surface joint, in which two flat faces or edges are butted up against each other, the abutment between the two parts only allows for the joint to be laid in position. There are various ways of making the joint secure: it can be assembled with wood glue, nails or screws, or a combination of these, such as glue and screws.

The butt joint rarely makes a direct contribution to the main construction of a

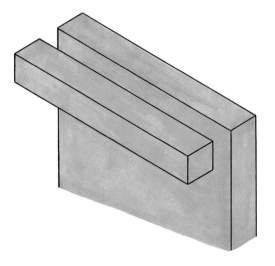

The butt joint.

The triangular corner block is reinforced with screws.

The three-sided joining block relies only on glue to provide its strength.

chair, but often takes a supporting role. One such example is the triangular corner joining block employed to attach a flat wooden seat on to its seat rails, or to reinforce the attachment of the seat rails to the legs of the chair and support a drop-in seat. It is also the butt joint that fixes a piece of moulding to the surface or edge for decorative effect.

Preparation of the butt joint is limited to cutting the wood to size and planing the surfaces to be joined until they are perfectly flat and thus able to make complete contact with each other. With corner joining blocks, the triangular shape means that the grain of the wood should run in the same direction as the base of the triangle, so that the two adjacent edges that butt up against the seat rails of the chair are cut at an angle to the grain. For a right-angled corner, both angles will be at 45 degrees to the grain. In the case of a corner

19

block used to join a seat to its rails, each block is cut lengthways and split or sawn into the appropriate triangle, so that each of the three faces lies equally with the grain.

THE MITRE JOINT

The mitre joint is formed by two pieces of wood having their ends cut at an angle of 45 degrees, so that they meet to form a right-angled corner. The angle may be varied to suit different types of work calling for larger or smaller angles, but the 90-degree mitre joint remains the most common.

In its simplest form, the two parts of the mitre joint are butted up together and assembled with wood glue, but as the area of the joining surface is usually somewhat limited, this method does not offer great strength and is only suitable if the joint is not subject to stresses or strains.

In chair-making, we usually associate the mitre joint with adding decorative mouldings. It is rarely a good idea to use the mitre joint in the main structure of a chair frame, but you will find it a useful adjunct to the mortise and tenon joint, where two tenons meet inside the chair leg and need to have their ends mitred, so that the two adjoining mortises can accommodate them satisfactorily.

There are two ways of preparing the simple mitre, which consists of no more than two lengths of wood with a 45-degree angle cut at one end. The first method is to measure out the position where each of the two angled cuts is to be made on its respective piece of wood, and mark across with a mitre square, which has its blade set at an angle of 45 degrees. Square across the two edges, and repeat the angle on the opposite side, always working from face-side and face-edge. Clamp the piece to the workbench, or hold it in a bench hook, and cut off the waste with the tenon saw. The angled cut can then be trimmed by placing the wood on a mitre shooting board and planing it smooth.

The second method starts in the same way, measuring the position of the joint on both lengths of wood, but, instead of marking with the mitre square, the two pieces are cut by placing them one at a time in a mitre box, lining them up with the 45-degree saw guides, and cutting them with the tenon saw. In either instance, you rely for accuracy on the use of a special jig – the shooting board or the mitre box. Both of these can be bought, or you can make your own.

The mitre joint.

Decorative moulding strips are mitred at their ends.

THE DOWEL JOINT

The dowel joint can take several forms, but in general it is similar to the butt joint except that it is precisely located and fastened by one or more lengths of wooden dowelling.

The purpose of the dowel, or peg, is to serve as a fixing pin, which is glued to both parts of the joint and thus locates them permanently in place. It has two important functions. First, it holds the joint firm against any tendency to pull apart, and second, it prevents the two joining surfaces from sliding laterally.

Since the dowels serve to reinforce what amounts to a simple butt joint, the overall effect is to secure the two pieces of wood doubly, with the butt joint taking effect by having glue applied along its entire joining surfaces. The dowel joint, therefore, offers potential for great strength. If the dowels only were to be glued, then the strength of the resulting joint would depend merely on the cross-sectional area of the dowels, which is small compared with the joint's total area.

The dowel joint is often regarded as one of the more recent innovations in woodwork,

acting as a substitute for the mortise and tenon joint in many contemporary designs, but it does have a long history of use, dating back to some of the earliest types of furniture. In fact, none of the chairs in this book uses the dowel joint in place of the mortise and tenon joint, but it is used to join panels together, and one particular chair is made of nothing but dowels.

Dowels are also used to provide decoration in the form of rails, and these are simply glued into receiver holes, usually of the stopped variety, which means that they do not pass right through the wood but are drilled to a pre-determined depth.

Dowelling is sold commercially in long lengths covering a range of standard diameters, and is usually made from the light-coloured hardwood called ramin. The most common sizes are 6mm (¼in), 9mm (⅜in), 13mm (½in), 16mm (⅝in) and 19mm (¾in). Occasionally you may find a slight discrepancy between the diameter of the dowel material and the drill bit, giving you a dowel that is either too loose in its hole or too big to fit. For this reason, it makes

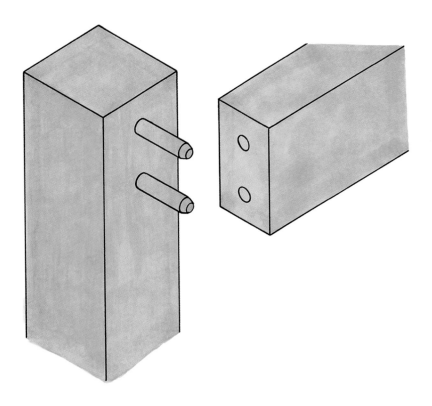

The dowel joint.

sense to carry out a trial run on a piece of scrap wood before you begin preparing your dowel joints in the workpiece. Ideally, the dowel should slide into its hole with no more than firm pressure from the fingers.

There are two distinct types of dowel joint that could be used in this book. The first of these is the joint that is used to assemble boards together, as in the case of the oak settle, where the dowel joint is combined with housing and lapped joint. The second type is the dowel joint, which serves as an alternative to the mortise and tenon joint, joining the end-grain of one piece to the edge or side of another, as in the construction of a chair frame. In fact, none of the chairs in this book uses dowel joints in these circumstances because the greater strength of the mortise and tenon joint is preferred, but it is always an option to be considered.

Taking the first example, the dowelling method is quite straightforward. Two solid boards of wood are to be joined together, where the end-grain of one board is to be fitted into a groove or rebate cut in the second board, with the two meeting at right-angles. Typically, the boards will measure 19mm (¾in) in thickness, so 6mm (¼in) diameter dowels are most appropriate for this purpose. To begin with, the boards are prepared with the housing joint groove, or the lapped joint rebate, and then the abutting surfaces are measured and marked for a series of matching dowel holes. If one board, 19mm (¾in) thick, has already had a 3mm (⅛in) deep groove or rebate cut in it, there is only scope to drill the holes for the dowels to a depth of 13mm (½in), otherwise each hole will pass right through the wood, which is not intended. You can drill deeper into the end-grain, of course, because there is a substantial amount of

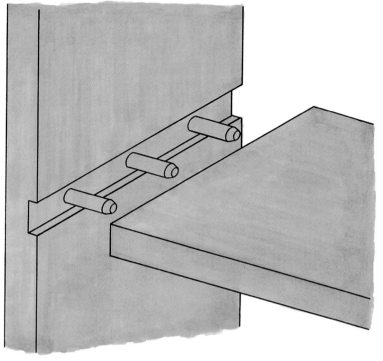

Exploded dowel joint.

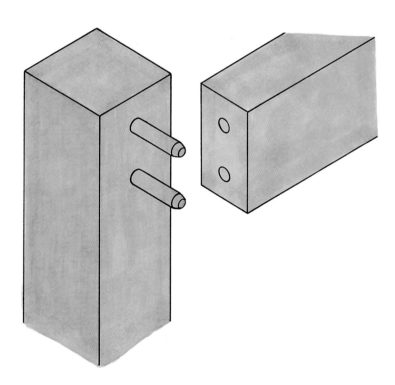

Exploded dowel joint.

wood behind it, although a depth of 25mm (1in) is quite adequate. The important point to bear in mind is that all of the holes should be drilled to a consistent depth. The dowels can then be cut to the same length, just under 38mm (1½in) in this instance. Chamfer their ends slightly by giving a couple of twists in a pencil sharpener to make it easier for them to engage in their receiver holes, and run the blade of the tenon saw along the length of each dowel to make a shallow channel, which allows for trapped air and glue to be expelled when the joint is fitted together.

In the second example, a dowel joint is formed between the edge of a chair leg and the end-grain of a rail. Two dowels are normally employed, but three or more may be required if the rail is especially deep. Mark and cut out a card template equal in size to the cross-sectional dimensions of the rail, as represented by the end-grain. Measure and draw a line along the centre of the template, and then set in the dowel positions. In deciding how near to the edges the dowels should be, as a rough guide you can divide the length of the template, that is the depth of the rail, into four parts, and

mark the dowels at the first and third intersections with the centre line.

When preparing to mark the dowel positions on the side or edge of the leg, it is a wise precaution to measure the leg so that it is slightly longer than necessary. In this way, you can avoid placing the template with its top edge lying flush with the end of the wood, and thus reduce the risk of the wood splitting when the top dowel hole is drilled. The same template is then carefully placed on the end-grain of the rail, which has already been cut perfectly square, and the dowel hole positions marked in each case. It is not always as easy to make a clear mark on end-grain in pencil, as would be the case for marking on the side or edge of the leg, so it is probably better to make the mark with a bradawl.

All of the dowel holes must be drilled with great precision. This is easily achieved with the holes in the leg by mounting the wood on a pillar drill. However, it is often rather difficult, when drilling into end-grain, to prevent the drill-bit from wandering off the mark, owing to the fibrous nature of the wood grain when approached end-on. Some of the denser woods

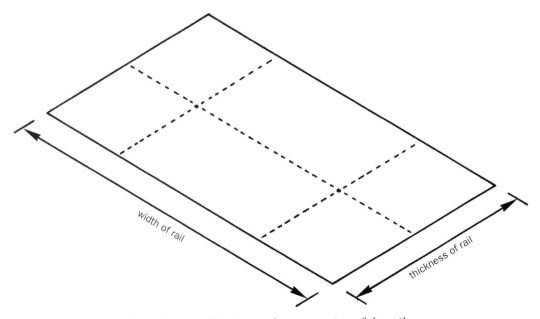

Mark and cut out a card template equal in size to the cross-section of the rail.

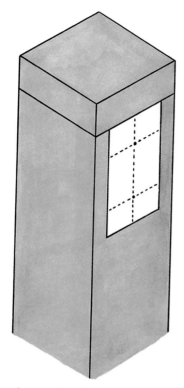

The template is placed on the leg in the position to be occupied by the rail.

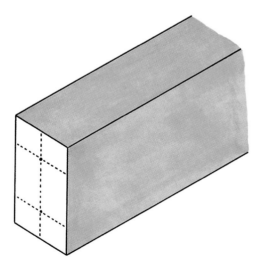

The same template is placed on the end-grain of the rail.

present little cause for concern, and the auger-bit makes a smooth, straight passage into the wood. For the looser-grained woods, it would be advisable to use a dowel-jig for absolute precision. Cut the leg to its correct length before assembling the joint. In this instance, each of the dowel holes should be at least 25mm (1in) deep, provided that the leg is sufficiently wide and thick.

THE HOUSING JOINT

The housing joint is formed by fitting the end of one piece of wood into a groove cut along the length, or across the grain, of the second piece, so that when the two parts are brought together they result in a recessed right-angled joint.

The simplest type of housing joint consists of a groove whose width is equal to the thickness of the wood that fits into it. The groove may either run for the full length or width of the piece in which it is cut, so that the recessed board is visible along both edges, or it can be stopped. When the groove occurs at the edge of the wood and resembles a rebate, the housing joint now takes the form of a lapped joint.

In another variation of the joint, the groove may be cut to a width less than the thickness of the wood that fits into it, in which case shoulders must be cut in the end of the joining piece, making for a more rigid, and less visible, joint. When this is taken to the extent of having a stopped groove cut in the first piece of wood, with a matching set of shoulders cut in the second piece that fits into the groove, you could well be forgiven for calling this a stopped four-shouldered mortise and tenon joint. Indeed, there are occasions when it is difficult to make the distinction between one joint and another.

The housing joint is used in the assembling of the bench settle and the oak settle, in which it plays a major part in the design of each chair, and in the fitting of the seat into the frame of the coffee-table chair.

To make a plain housing joint, take the piece of wood in which the groove is to be cut and

25

The housing joint.

check that its surface is perfectly flat. The board that fits into the groove must have its end marked and cut square, and the end-grain cleaned up with the plane. Measure the thickness of the board as accurately as possible, and use this distance to set the width of the groove, squaring across the surface of the wood and scribing two parallel lines with the blade of a marking knife. Continue the marking of the lines around both edges in pencil, unless the joint is of the stopped variety, in which case it does not reach the edges of the wood. Determine the depth of the groove: it may be up to one-third the thickness of the wood in which it is to be cut, or it could be less, depending on the circumstances of the joint.

The quickest and most effective way of cutting the groove is to use the electric router, using a length of straight-edged batten to act as a guide for the tool. For a groove that runs the entire length or width of the wood, it may alternatively be cut by sawing along the two marked lines, down to the pre-determined depth, and chopping out the waste with the chisel. When all of the waste has been removed, by whichever means, fit the end of the board into its groove. The two parts should fit together with firm hand pressure.

For the cutting of the housing joint in a seat rail, as for the coffee-table chair, the groove is firstly marked on one face of the wood with a mortise gauge and, instead of cutting the rails up into their individual lengths, the wood is marked as a single long piece, clamped securely to the top of the workbench, and the groove cut in one go with the router.

THE HALVED JOINT

The halved joint, or lapped joint as it is also known, is used to join together two lengths of wood, usually at right-angles, by removing half the thickness from both pieces so that when they are brought into contact their surfaces remain flush. The joint can either be located along the length of the wood, or at the end of it.

There is not much call for the halved joint in chair-making, and its brief appearance in this book is confined to the method of joining the decorative edge pieces to the solid wood seat of the pine dining-chair, in order to conceal the end-grain. Each part of the joint is, in fact, a rebate, both being of equal dimensions, cut with an electric router.

THE MORTISE AND TENON JOINT

This is one of the most common and important joints in woodwork, and is the joint used most often in chair-making. It consists of a mortise, or opening, cut into one piece of wood, and a tenon, or tongue, equal in size to the mortise, cut at the end of the second piece. It possesses

great potential strength, can be adapted to a wide variety of uses and, in the majority of cases, remains well-concealed inside the wood. Its strength lies in the fact that the joining surfaces cover a relatively large area over which the wood glue can act.

There are a number of variations to this versatile joint. For example, some tenons are cut with two shoulders, while others are more refined with four. Those that have only one main shoulder are known as bare-faced tenons. Some mortises pass right through the wood to come out on the opposite side or edge, called 'through mortises'. Others stop short within the wood and are not visible from outside; these are called 'stopped mortises'. There are also the haunched and mitred tenons.

For greatest strength, the assembled joints are held firm with dowel pegs. When pegs are fitted, the hole in the tenon is usually off-set slightly from the mortise hole so that the insertion of the peg pulls the joint tightly together, a process known as 'draw-boring'.

The mortise and tenon joint occurs in such a wide variety of circumstances that it is virtually

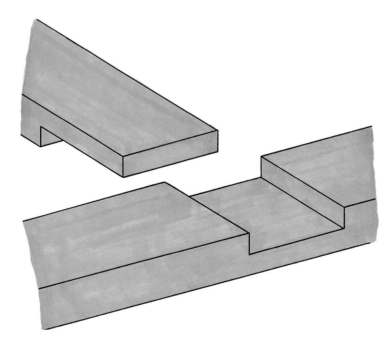

The halved joint.

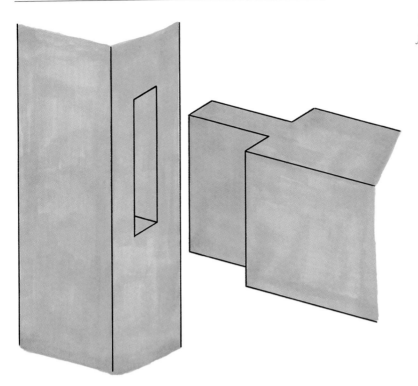

The mortise and tenon joint.

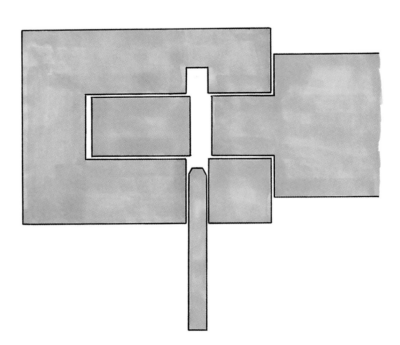

The draw-boring technique, seen in cross-section.

impossible to say that any one situation is typical. Having said that, there are certain features that lend one particular type of mortise and tenon joint to one particular application, and it may be stated that chair-making generally makes use of the four-shouldered stopped mortise and tenon.

The theory of the mortise and tenon joint is that the mortise, and therefore the tenon, should be equal to one-third the thickness of the wood in which they are cut. This holds up perfectly when both parts of the joint are prepared from pieces of the same thickness, but it often so happens that the design requires that one piece should be thicker than the other: the leg of a chair is normally of a greater thickness than the rail. It is usual to arrange for the mortise and tenon to be as large as possible, so the one-third rule is applied to the greater thickness, which in most cases is that of the leg. Assuming that the rail is not less than one-third the leg thickness, a tenon can still be cut successfully, even though it has shallower shoulders.

For simplicity, in the following description of how to make the joint, let us assume that the mortise and tenon are to be cut from pieces of equal width and thickness. First, check that the sides and edges are all planed straight and square. Even when the wood has been supplied

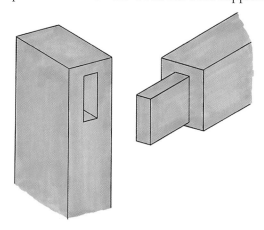

The four-shouldered stopped mortise and tenon joint.

by the local timber merchant to your own specified dimensions, it is still wise to run the tape measure over each individual piece to ensure that it is of the required width and thickness.

Start by marking in the position of the mortise. When it is to be set close to the end of the wood, as when joining a seat rail to a front chair leg, allow at least 25mm (1in) extra to serve as a safety margin, so that when the mortise is being cut there is sufficient wood to prevent the piece from splitting. After the mortise has been cut, and before the joint is fitted together, this surplus is trimmed. There is no need to allow a safety margin for a mortise placed along the length of the wood, because enough material exists at both ends of the joint.

Mark out with the tape-measure, square and pencil. Measure the distance from the end of the wood and square two lines across the edge of the piece where you want to make the mortise, separating the lines by an amount equal to the width of the rail in which the tenon will be cut. Continue squaring the lines around the wood.

Set the distance between the two spurs of a mortise gauge to the width of the chisel that is nearest in size to one-third the thickness of the wood, and adjust the fence of the gauge until the two spurs make a pair of tiny impressions centrally on the edge. You can easily check whether or not the two points are dead-centre by holding the fence against each of the opposing sides in turn. When the pair of impressions coincide from both directions, you know that they are precisely in the middle. Having said that, it is still advisable to work the gauge from the face-side for all marking operations. Run the gauge along the edge of the wood so that the two spurs inscribe a pair of parallel lines between the two squared pencil lines.

As the tenon is to have four shoulders, the next task is to measure and mark the setting in of the mortise at each end. These amounts depend on where the mortise is situated. For example, when the mortise is positioned very

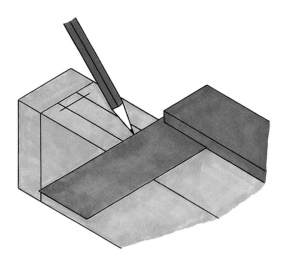

Mark a pair of parallel lines with the mortise gauge between the two squared pencil lines.

The mortise is inset at each end, so that it is entirely concealed from view in the finished joint.

near to the end of the wood, the distance must be sufficient to prevent the end-grain from breaking away when the tenon is fitted. But the other end of the mortise needs only a small setting in, just enough to prevent the tenon from being visible when the joint is assembled. If the mortise is to be placed along the length of the wood, far removed from either end-grain, it only needs to be set in by a small amount at both ends.

Decide how much of an inset you require, and measure this distance at the two ends of the mortise with the tape measure, marking with the pencil and squaring across the edge of the piece. The mortise has now assumed the shape of a clearly defined box, bounded by a pair of inscribed lines from the mortise gauge and squared pencil lines.

One further point to consider is how far down into the wood the mortise should be cut. The generally accepted rule for a stopped mortise is that it should be equal in depth to three-quarters the thickness of the piece in which it is cut, although this is a somewhat arbitrary figure. Also, chair legs have mortises cut in adjacent sides, to accommodate seat rails, and these often meet within the wood.

Although it is perfectly feasible to remove all of the waste from the mortise with the chisel and mallet, this is an unnecessarily long, drawn-out task. To speed up the process, much of the waste may be drilled out by boring a series of holes along the length of the mortise. It is important that the drill-bit should be slightly smaller in diameter than the width of the mortise, so that each drilled hole fits comfortably within the scribed lines. The pillar drill is an excellent tool for this purpose, since it is fitted with its own depth-gauge to measure precisely the depth of each hole, and thus the mortise.

Chop out the remainder of the waste with the chisel and mallet. Starting near the centre, the first chisel cuts are made with the chisel inclined at an angle so that, when worked from both directions, the cutting forms a V-shape. As you progress deeper and further back towards the two ends of the mortise, you should gradually bring the chisel up to the vertical. Stop fractionally short of the two squared end lines, because as you prise out waste from the deepest part of the mortise, you will find that the levering action of the chisel makes a dent in the wood. Once the mortise has been almost

30

completely chopped out, you may then place the chisel blade on each of the two end lines and, with the tool held absolutely vertical, strike hard with the mallet to make a final downward cut to complete the mortise.

To mark and cut out the tenon, begin by taking the measurement for the depth of the mortise, and transfer slightly less than this distance to the end of the piece in which the tenon is to be prepared. Square right around the wood at this point, working the square from the face-side and face-edge. With the mortise gauge set as previously, scribe the two parallel lines along the two edges and the end-grain of the wood, working the gauge from the face-side for all three pairs of lines. Remember that if a rail is narrower than the leg, as is often the case in chair construction, the mortise gauge fence will need to be adjusted to centralize the lines for the tenon.

Clamp the wood in the workbench vice at an angle of approximately 45 degrees, and cut on the waste side of the marked lines with the tenon saw as far down as the squared shoulder line. Turn the piece around and repeat the same cut from the opposite edge. Finally, holding it in an upright position in the vice, saw straight down.

Remove the piece from the vice and, laying it flat on the workbench, place the square against each of the shoulder lines pencilled across the two sides of the wood, and score along both lines with the marking knife. Hold the piece firmly in the bench hook, or clamp it horizontally in the vice, and cut down on the waste side of the marked lines to remove the shoulders.

The next stage is to cut the third and fourth shoulders to match the setting in at both ends of the mortise. Place the rail in position with respect to the leg and make pencil marks on the tenon to indicate where the two ends of the mortise occur. Mark in these lines along the length of the tenon with the pencil and ruler. A special technique employed by experienced woodworkers is to grip the pencil so that the tips of your fingers press against the edge of the

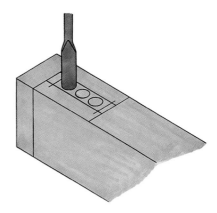

Most of the waste is removed from the mortise by drilling a series of holes along its length.

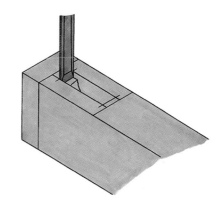

The remainder of the waste is chopped out from the mortise with the chisel.

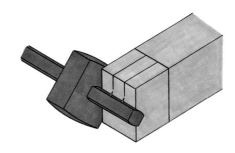

The mortise gauge marks an identical pair of parallel lines for the tenon.

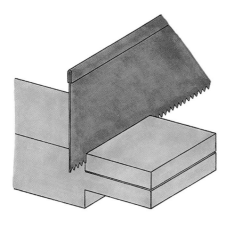

Cut off the two main portions of waste with the tenon saw.

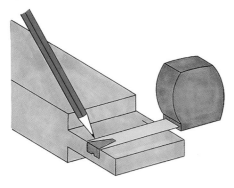

Measure and mark in the positions of the third and fourth shoulders to match the setting in at both ends of the mortise.

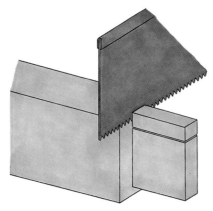

Complete the cutting of the third and fourth shoulders.

wood, and run your hand up and down the length of the tenon to make a straight line with the pencil's point.

Clamp the piece upright in the vice again and saw down the lines as far as the main shoulder line, then re-position it horizontally and complete cutting off the waste to create the second pair of shoulders.

The tenon should now fit fully into the mortise with only a light tapping of the mallet. If resistance is felt, remove the tenon from the mortise, and, where you can see shiny marks on the cheeks of the tenon caused by the binding of the surfaces, gently pare off a few shavings of wood with the chisel, trimming until the tenon fits perfectly.

The stopped mortise and tenon joint is assembled with wood glue, the glue being applied to all of the joining surfaces with a brush, and the two parts tapped together and cramped securely for the duration of the glue's drying time.

The pegging of a mortise and tenon joint is favoured for certain types of work. The dowel peg has been in use since the earliest days of woodwork, although with the advent of powerful synthetic wood glues, the need for the peg has somewhat diminished, but it still retains one important function: the process known as draw-boring.

In draw-boring, holes are bored through the sides of the mortise and tenon. This is done so that, with the hole in the tenon being slightly off-set from those in the mortise, when a dowel peg is driven in it serves to draw the tenon further into the joint. The result is a very secure fixture.

A small or medium-sized joint will only require one peg, but a large joint will need two. The dowels may be 6mm (¼in) or 9mm (⅜in) in diameter, and their receiver holes are drilled with matching bits.

The positioning of the hole, or holes, is not critical, but you should aim for it to be somewhere near the centre of the tenon cheek for a single peg, or spaced regularly apart for two pegs, with plenty of tenon on either side.

Once the positions have been roughly determined on the tenon, it is a simple matter to transfer these by measurement to the side of the mortise. Although the drilled hole must pass right through the mortise and into the wood on the other side, it must not be allowed to break through on the opposite surface of the wood. Fit the tenon into the mortise, and mark the position of the hole, then remove the tenon again and set the position of the hole 2mm (³⁄₃₂in) nearer to the tenon's shoulder, drilling right through it.

Cut the dowel peg to length and chamfer the end that is to be driven into the hole so that it has the ability to push its way into the off-set tenon without baulking, as would be the case if the end were left square. The pegged mortise and tenon joint is glued together but, due to the pulling effect of the draw-boring technique, there is no need to cramp up the assembly.

The mitred tenon is used when two rails are joined at right-angles to the same leg, so that the two stopped mortises combine with one another deep inside the wood. If each tenon were cut to fit its own mortise, a part of it would block the entry of the other – so the problem is resolved by cutting 45-degree mitre joints at the end of both tenons, enabling each one to fit fully into its own mortise without interfering with the other.

There is no point in trying to arrange for the mitred surfaces to meet and touch inside the joint, since little additional strength will be gained in comparison with the overall effectiveness of the mortise and tenon joint.

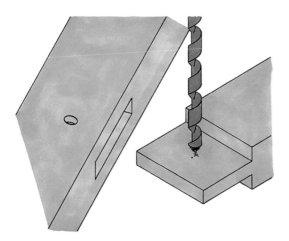

Draw-boring – drilling the off-set hole through the tenon.

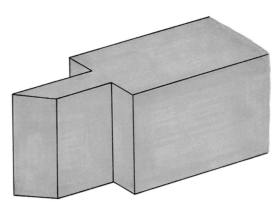

A mitred tenon.

The finished spider seat, closed.

The finished spider seat, open.

34

CHAPTER 4

The Spider Seat

The spider seat is a child's curiosity, something to provide amusement in the corner of the bedroom or playroom. Many children have a fear of real spiders, particularly large black ones with eight huge legs, but when the creature is transformed into an inanimate object with big bright eyes and a charming smile, all thoughts of terror are banished. The spider's head and body are the back of the seat, folded flat to become a stool, but as soon as the seat is lifted up, it becomes the back of the chair, revealing a smaller seat underneath, to which the eight legs are attached.

Two materials are used to make this unusual seat: plywood and dowelling. The three component parts of the seat are cut from high-quality birch-faced plywood measuring 16mm (⅝in) thick and the legs are 25mm (1in) diameter ramin dowelling. The jointing is straightforward, with the two main parts of the seat butted up against each other and glued together, the eight legs fitted into 25mm (1in) diameter holes, and the seat back hinged in place with two ordinary mild steel door hinges.

Anyone who is knowledgeable about spiders will realize that there is a small flaw in the design, for real spiders have their eight legs attached to the head section, whereas in this instance they come from the abdomen, or the spider's body.

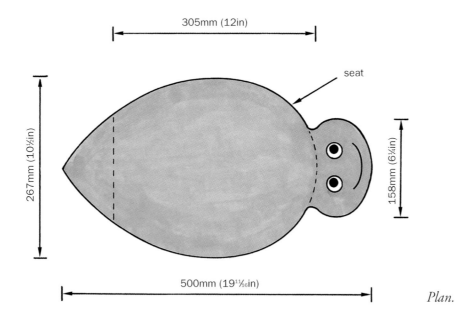

305mm (12in)

seat

267mm (10½in)

158mm (6¼in)

500mm (19¹¹⁄₁₆in)

Plan.

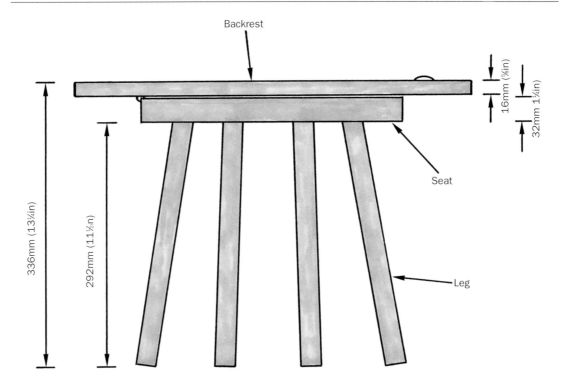

Backrest

16mm (⅝in)

32mm 1¼in)

Seat

336mm (13¼in)

292mm (11½in)

Leg

Side elevation.

Mark out the shape of the spider on a large piece of paper, which will serve as a template. If you fold the paper in half to begin with, and draw in half a head and body, when the pattern is cut out and unfolded, the resulting shape will be symmetrical as it ought to be. Transfer the pattern three times on to a sheet of birch-faced plywood and cut out with the jigsaw. It is best to fit the jigsaw with a fine wood-cutting blade for the best result, but even so, the fast up-and-down action of the blade can rip away pieces of ply from the top layer, leading to a rather ragged edge, even though the underside is cut perfectly. To avoid this kind of damage from occurring, first mark around the drawn pencil line with a sharp knife and work the jigsaw blade just on the waste side of this cut-mark. When you come to cut out the second and third of the three patterns, you could use the first example as your template, holding it down

on to the plywood sheet with firm pressure and working the jigsaw blade carefully around it.

By the time the cutting out is completed, you should have three identical spider shapes, but only one is needed in its entirety. The other two need to have the head and the tail cut away to form the seat, and this is achieved by going back to the original paper template and modifying it with a curve at the head end and a straight edge, at right-angles to the fold, at the back. Following the same procedure as for the cutting out of the first shape, score a line along

---

The Spider Seat Cutting List

Seat: Three of 500 × 275 × 16mm (19¹¹⁄₁₆ × 10¹³⁄₁₆ × ⅝in) plywood

Leg: Eight of 305 × 25mm (12 × 1in) dowelling

The shape of the spider is transferred from the template on to the plywood.

Cutting out the seat with the jigsaw.

The head and rear end of the body are removed from the two seat pieces.

the pencil markings with the sharp knife, and cut away the waste with the jigsaw. You are left with the full-sized folding down backrest, and two smaller but identical seats, one of which will be affixed on to the top of the other.

The eight spider legs are each cut to a length of 305mm (12in), which is actually a contrived length because the 25mm (1in) diameter dowelling is supplied in lengths of 2,440mm (8ft), so it is simply cut up into eight equal parts. The legs are fitted into receiver holes cut in the underside of the seat. The marking and cutting of these holes requires a great deal of care, because correct positioning of the legs is necessary for safety and stability. Furthermore, each leg should be splayed outwards, and the angle of splay must be consistent. To begin with the marking of the leg positions, go back again to the paper template, fold it in half along its crease and pencil in the position of four legs, arranging them evenly apart, and setting their centres 38mm (1½in) from the edge. Once you are satisfied that they are placed correctly, press the point of a small nail or panel pin through each of the four pencil markings so that when you unfold the paper, you are left with all eight leg positions.

Take the lower plywood seat panel, turn it upside-down and lay the template on to it, in perfect alignment, and mark in the eight hole positions with the point of a pencil. Remove the template, and ensure that the pencil marks can be clearly seen, by going over them again if necessary. The most accurate method of drilling the eight holes is to use the pillar drill, for not only has this got a depth-gauge, which will permit you to drill all the holes to exactly the same depth, but also the workpiece rest, which normally lies horizontally, may be tilted to any chosen angle, so that each leg can be given the same degree of splay. The angle selected for this example is 10 degrees.

If you do not have access to a pillar drill, the holes can be drilled easily enough manually, using either a hand-drill or brace fitted with a 25mm (1in) diameter wood-cutting bit. You will either have to estimate the desired angle by

Marking the eight leg positions using the template.

Gluing the legs into their holes.

Each of the leg holes is angled to give a splay to the legs, and bored out with the pillar drill.

The hingeing arrangement.

guesswork, or place an adjustable try-square against it, set to 10 degrees, or whatever. Drill each of the eight holes to a depth of 16mm (⅝in) or less, where the drill-bit is just about to break through on the other side of the ply, and clean out the holes to ensure that they are equal.

Place the identical top seat panel in position against the bottom panel to check that their adjoining surfaces lie perfectly in contact – the drilling of the eight holes could have caused raised bumps where the drill-bit just broke the surface, in which case these should all be rubbed flat with sandpaper – and when you are

satisfied that the two seat components butt together precisely, apply glue to both parts, assemble and place to one side while the glue dries and sets hard. It would be a good idea to lay a heavy object on top of the assembly, such as a brick, to maintain firm pressure on the joint during the drying process.

Once the two seat halves are firmly bonded together, rub down the curved edges with medium-grade sandpaper to produce a smooth finish, and repeat the same procedure for the straight edge at the back.

Turn the completed seat assembly upside-down again, apply wood glue to the eight holes and fit the legs in position. There will probably be a small amount of movement of the legs inside their holes, so this is the time to check that the legs are all correctly and evenly placed, before the glue dries.

The backrest is hinged to the seat with two 63mm (2½in) mild steel butt hinges, cutting shallow rebates in both surfaces to recess both parts of each hinge. Normally a hinge is screwed into place, and indeed, this is a perfectly acceptable way of attaching the two hinges to the seat, which measures 32mm (1¼in) thick, but the backrest is only 16mm (⅝in) thick, and short screws might not hold it securely enough, so nuts and bolts are the answer here, with the holes for the bolts recessed slightly to conceal the nuts from view, the recesses being plugged with a suitable wood-filler after the hinges are fitted.

Sandpaper the spider thoroughly, paying particular attention to the rounding off of the edges. Mark in a face on the head. You can purchase large plastic eyes from sewing and craft shops: those used in this example measure 25mm (1in) in diameter and have black pupils that move about inside. They require a shallow 6mm (¼in) diameter hole to be drilled in the plywood to receive them. The mouth is a big crescent, marked in pencil and cut out with a chisel or gouge.

Paint the spider matt black, except for the mouth, which is painted a glossy white, and give a thorough application of clear satin varnish. When completely dry, glue the eyes in place, and the friendly spider is ready for use.

The finished bedroom chair.

CHAPTER 5

The Bedroom Chair

This unusual bedroom chair combines two separate and distinct features to create a design that is bold and daring: everything about its overall appearance is to do with squareness, and yet all of the constituent parts are round, for it is made entirely from dowelling and mopstick. This is a painted chair, with no attempt made to bring out the texture of the wood; a pure white serves instead to capture and hold the attention. If it seems more likely that the bedroom calls for a softly padded seat, how could you possibly conceal the concentric diamond pattern upon which you sit? And yet this is not some impractical chair merely to look at – it is a chair that fulfils its purpose but is a little secretive and daring.

The design is simple and the method of construction straightforward, making this one of the easiest chairs to build, involving the most basic of joints: butt joints, mitre joints and dowel joints. It is made with four different diameters of dowelling: the legs are 45mm (1⅛in) in diameter, and may be cut either from perfectly round dowel, or mopstick, a cheaper version in softwood, with a flattened edge, often used as handrail material. The four main seat rails and the two bottom rails are 25mm (1in) dowels, the seat and its supports 19mm (¾in) dowels, and the backrest and stretcher rails 13mm (½in) dowels.

Cut the mopstick to length for all four legs. Measure and mark in the dowel hole positions in each of the four legs for the top and bottom rails – you should aim to mark in the centre of the dowel holes at the point where the drill-bit touches the wood, halfway across its diameter.

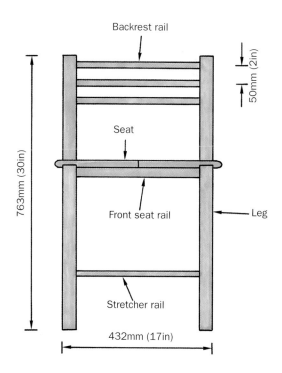

Front elevation.

Since accuracy is such an important characteristic of this joint, the drilling of the holes needs to be carried out with great precision, and this is clearly a case where the pillar drill, or a vertical drill-stand, is essential. Fit a 25mm (1in) diameter wood-cutting bit into the chuck of the drill, set the depth gauge to 19mm (¾in), and commence drilling the holes. The holes for the four main seat rails will coincide to some extent, but you are not advised to drill any

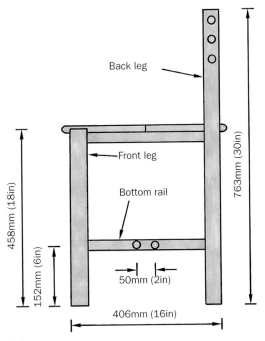

Back leg

Front leg

Bottom rail

458mm (18in)

152mm (6in)

763mm (30in)

50mm (2in)

406mm (16in)

Side elevation.

The Bedroom Chair Cutting List	
Front leg:	Two of 458 × 45mm (18 × 1¾in)
Back leg:	Two of 762 × 45mm (30 × 1¾in)
Front seat rail:	One of 388 × 25mm (15¼ × 1in)
Back seat rail:	One of 388 × 25mm (15¼ × 1in)
Side seat rail:	Two of 360 × 25mm (14³⁄₁₆ × 1in)
Bottom rail:	Two of 360 × 25mm (14³⁄₁₆ × 1in)
Backrest rail:	Three of 388 × 13mm (15¼ × ½in)
Stretcher rail:	Two of 394 × 13mm (15½ × ½in)
Long seat support:	One of 353 × 19mm (13⅞ × ¾in)
Short seat support:	Two of 184 × 19mm (7¼ × ¾in)
Outer seat:	Four of 305 × 19mm (12 × ¾in)
Middle seat:	Four of 202 × 19mm (8 × ¾in)
Inner seat:	Four of 100 × 19mm (4 × ¾in)

The dowel joint holes are bored in each component with the pillar drill.

deeper than 19mm (¾in) because to do so would risk compromising the strength of the mopstick.

Cut all six rails to length, allowing for the 19mm (¾in) extra at each end which fits into the holes. Note that the two bottom rails are cut square, whereas the four top rails need to have their ends partially mitred so that they butt tightly up against each other at right-angles inside the joints. To determine how much mitring is required, push each dowel rail into its hole, one at a time, and mark in pencil the point where it coincides with its adjacent dowel hole. Rather than saw off the waste in a mitre block, which could rip away some of the ramin from the surface, simply remove the waste by paring it off with a chisel. The point to watch out for here is that once you have cut the mitre at one end, the opposite end must be mitred in a corresponding position, otherwise you will finish up with a chair that is off-square.

Mark in the positions of the three backrest rails

*Assembling one of the
chair sides.*

*The cruciform support
fitted in place.*

*Assembling the seat
squares.*

at the top of each back leg, and the two stretcher rails midway along each bottom rail. In each instance, these are set 50mm (2in) apart from one another, and the holes drilled with a 13mm (½in) wood-cutting bit mounted in the pillar drill, boring to a depth of 19mm (¾in) in the back legs and 13mm (½in) in the bottom rails.

Cut the three backrest rails and two stretcher rails to length, and do a trial run of the assembly, without glue, to make sure that all the dowels fit into their respective holes. This is not an easy task and may require more than one pair of hands. For the final assembly, introduce plenty of wood glue into each of the dowel holes and tap them fully together, wiping away excess glue from the surfaces with a damp cloth. If you are working alone, without anyone to assist, you will undoubtedly find the task much more manageable by assembling the two sides first, leaving these to dry and harden, before introducing the two remaining seat rails, the backrest and the stretcher rails. Make sure, during the assembly process, that the chair stands square, each leg in contact with a flat surface, so that if you need to make any slight adjustments, these can be carried out before the glue has set hard.

The seat, with its pattern of three squares, arranged concentrically, is made entirely from 19mm (¾in) diameter dowelling. Begin by cutting the four components for each square, with a 45-degree mitre at each end. Once again,

make certain that each mitre corresponds precisely with the other. The length of each side is 305mm (12in) for the largest square, 200mm (8in) for the middle square and 100mm (4in) for the smallest square. Apply wood glue to each mitre and assemble the squares, standing each one on a flat surface to dry.

A cruciform support, which runs between the centres of each seat rail, is made likewise from 19mm (¾in) dowelling. One member, which runs in a single length from front to back, is shaped at each end with a 25mm (1in) diameter curve applied to it with the 25mm (1in) wood-drilling bit mounted in the pillar drill. This is quite a difficult cut to achieve, and you would be advised to practise first on some scrap dowelling.

The side-to-side members, two of them, are cut with a 25mm (1in) diameter curve at each of their outer ends, and a 19mm (¾in) diameter curve where they meet up with the front to back member to form the cross. When you are satisfied that they fit together properly, glue them in place. The squares for the seat are then arranged, diamond-wise, on the rails and glued in position.

It only remains to paint the chair in the chosen colour and it is finished.

Mitring the end of a seat rail with the chisel.

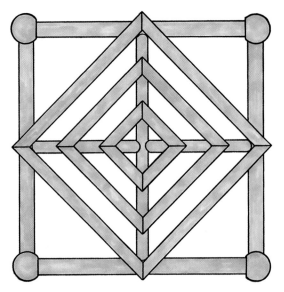

The seat pattern.

CHAPTER 6

The Bench Settle

An early form of seat is the open bench, but if this idea is modified so that the ends are extended upwards into sides, and a plain backrest added, the result is a type of settle, somewhat reminiscent of a church pew in that the main parts of the seat are put together with mortise and tenon joints, where the tenons pass right through the mortises and are fixed with pegs or tusks. If the bench settle is made from pine, it is an easy and quite inexpensive chair that will fit in well with other pine furniture, especially in the kitchen or dining room.

Although the term pine is used, this particular example was built from whitewood, which is a cheap material characterized by plenty of small knots. Its main advantage is that it is used in the making of tongued-and-grooved floorboards, and this is ideally suited to our purpose. The two sides, the seat and the backrest are all cut from solid wide boards and,

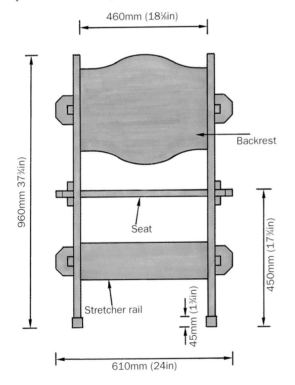

Front elevation.

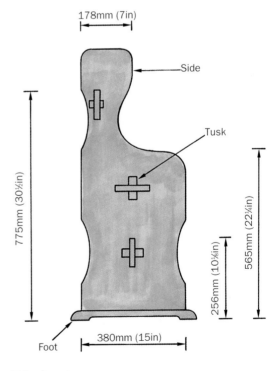

Side elevation.

The finished bench settle.

unless you obtain these from old salvaged wood from broken-up furniture, as shown in the next chapter, you will have to make the boards yourself. Of course, you could choose any type of wood you want and joint the planks into wide boards by cutting your own tongues and grooves, but this seems an opportunity not to be missed: simply go to your local timber stockist and ask for some 150 × 25mm (6 × 1in) tongued-and-grooved floorboard material. What you end up with is not 'six-by-one' at all, it is more like 140 × 19mm (5½ × ¾in) after it has been planed, but this measurement includes the tongue. The two sides, the seat and the backrest are each made up of three tongued-and-grooved floorboards with their joints glued together: the two sides both measure 915mm (36in) in length, and the seat and the backrest 610mm (24in) each. Similarly, the bottom stretcher rail is 610mm (24in) long, but this is made from a single piece of material with the tongue and groove planed off, bringing it to a width of 125mm (5in).

Once all of the boards have been glued together and assembled so that the joins are barely visible, leave for at least a day to ensure that the glue has completely set, and then plane down the tongues and grooves from the edges so that you end up with side panels that are

380mm (15in) wide, and a seat and backrest that are each 368mm (14½in) wide. Of these, only the seat retains its straight edges, the others need to be shaped with curves.

It is up to you whether you want to prepare templates, or draw the curves freehand with some assistance from drawing instruments. If you wish to make a set of identical bench settles, a card or thin plywood template would be a good idea, for this would ensure consistency

The Bench Settle Cutting List	
Side:	Two of 915 × 380 × 19mm (36 × 15 × ¾in)
Seat:	One of 610 × 368 × 19mm (24 × 14½ × ¾in)
Backrest:	One of 610 × 368 × 19mm (24 × 14½ × ¾in)
Stretcher rail:	One of 610 × 125 × 19mm (24 × 5 × ¾in)
Foot:	Two of 458 × 45 × 32mm (18 × 1¾ × 1¼in)
Long tusk:	Four of 75 × 25 × 19mm (3 × 1 × ¾in)
Short tusk:	Two of 50 × 25 × 19mm (2 × 1 × ¾in)

Cutting out one of the side-panels with the jigsaw.

throughout. I marked mine out more or less freehand, using a tape measure to maintain accuracy between front and back edge, and to measure how deeply to mark in the curves, and then I cut out the first side-panel with the jigsaw and used this as a pattern for the second. I then took one of the waste portions from the curve cut-outs, and used this to mark the curves on the top and bottom edges of the backrest. It was as simple as that!

The bottom edge of the two side panels will eventually have a foot attached, but for the time being it is sufficient to cut and plane each end straight and square. It is important to ensure that both sides are identical, and this will mean clamping them together in the workbench vice, perfectly aligned along their bottom edges, trimming the curves with the spokeshave and sandpapering the edges smooth until they are exactly the same. It only remains to inspect the outer surfaces of the two sides in order to determine which should face outwards and which should face inwards. It would obviously be preferable for the better surface to face outwards, whether this means the surface with the fewer knots, the better grain pattern or the closer fitting joins between the tongues and grooves. In actual fact there ought not to be much difference between the surfaces anyway, otherwise you should not have bought the wood in the first place, but insisted on better quality material!

Because the side-panels are so large, and have irregular edges, it is impossible to mark in the positions for the seat, backrest and stretcher rail with any form of gauge, but you must rely instead on accurate measurement with the tape measure, pencil and a long straight edge. The seat and backrest are both fitted in place with a combination of mortise and tenon, and housing joint, where the mortise and tenon occupies the middle 125mm (5in) of the seat and 100mm (4in) of the backrest, with the remainder housed in a shallow groove, except for the final 25mm (1in) at each end. If this sounds unduly complicated, it is not, because the mortise and tusk tenon provides the fixing of the joint in a manner that is visually acceptable, and the housing groove makes certain that the rest of the two boards' widths do not bend out of shape, which could happen if they were left unsupported. So really each joint consists of a 6mm (¼in) deep housing groove, 19mm (¾in) wide, which, in the middle, passes right

The electric router is used to cut out the housing channels.

through the wood to form a mortise.

The bottom stretcher rail is a straightforward mortise, with no housing groove at all, measuring 100mm (4in) long, giving an inset of 13mm (½in) for each of the tenon shoulders.

Measure and mark in the joint positions on the inside surfaces of both side panels, checking that they are compatible with one another. Remember that each housing groove is set in by 25mm (1in) at both ends. The waste should be removed with the electric router, guiding this against a piece of straight-edged batten clamped to the panel. Make several passes with a 6mm (¼in) wide cutter, working this to a depth of 6mm (¼in), cutting the ends square with the chisel. Then mark in the mortise position in the centre of the groove, again removing the waste with the router, this time set to a depth of 19mm (¾in) where it should just break through on the other side of the panel. Clean out the last vestiges of waste with the chisel, taking care not to damage the outside surface. The same procedure may be repeated for the stretcher rail mortise, which has no housing element.

It has already been stated that the seat is fitted as it is, with straight front and back edges, but the backrest should have been marked with curves, and if these have not already been cut, this is the time to do it. Remove the bulk of the waste with the jigsaw, completing the smooth flow of the curves with the spokeshave and finishing with sandpaper.

The tenons and tongues should now be marked in at the ends of the seat and backrest. The distance between the inside faces of the side panels is 458mm (18in), and the tongues are 6mm (¼in) deep, the remainder being the tenons. Check and double-check your markings before attempting to cut away the waste, for a mistake at this stage would entail having to make a new seat or backrest, but when you are satisfied that the positioning is correct, cut off the waste with the jigsaw. The tenons at the ends of the stretcher are simpler to cut, since there are no tongues, and the stretcher measures 458mm (18in) plus each tenon.

Make a trial fitting of each joint, individually to begin with, in order to ascertain that the parts slot fully into place. If there is any tendency for the joints to bind, or not fit properly, determine where the problem lies and remedy the matter, so that eventually a complete assembly can be made with everything fitting perfectly together. For final assembly, the joints will be pegged with wooden tusks, cut from softwood measuring 25×19mm ($1 \times \frac{3}{4}$in) in cross-section.

Mark in the tusk position for each tenon, doing the equivalent of a draw-boring exercise, where the tusk is set 2mm (³⁄₃₂in) nearer to the tenon's shoulder, so that it pulls the joint more tightly together during assembly. Cut the waste from the tusk position, rather in the manner of making another mortise and, for neatness,

Cutting a tusk hole in the backrest.

Fitting a foot to a side-panel with a dowel joint.

A tusk is offered up to its hole. The forward inside edge of each tusk is chamfered slightly to prevent baulking as it is knocked into its hole.

Assembling the bench settle.

mark a diagonal line at each corner of the tenon and saw off the waste, to give a softer appearance.

Take the assembly apart and prepare the two feet that are fitted at the bottom of the sides. These are pieces of softwood, measuring 45 × 32mm (1¾ × 1¼in) in cross-section, 458mm (18in) in length, with rounded ends and a section removed from the bottom edge to a depth of 13mm (½in), set in by 63mm (2½in) from each end. These two feet are attached to the bottom edge of the sides with dowel joints, three 9mm (⅜in) dowels per joint, each receiver

hole bored to a depth of 25mm (1in), the dowels measuring 45mm (1¾in) each. Apply wood glue to the dowels and their holes, with a small amount of glue run along the end-grain of the side panels, and assemble the feet, wiping any surplus glue away.

When the glue is dry, prepare for the final assembling of the bench settle. No glue is used at all for the main joints, relying instead on the pegging of the tenons. Cut six tusks, those for the seat and stretcher rail measuring 75mm (3in) in length, the pair for the backrest being only 50mm (2in) long. Chamfer one inside edge for each tusk, so that it will fit more easily through its receiver hole, and knock it fully into place using the mallet and a short length of scrap wood as a drift. The tusks need to be a tight fit if the joints are to be firm, but the advantage with this type of assembly is that if they loosen over the course of time, new tusks can be fitted in their place. Wedged tusks merely need to be driven in further.

Apply a light oak wood stain and finish with two coats of matt or satin clear varnish.

CHAPTER 7

The Oak Settle

The old-fashioned settle, once found in country inns and such places, is particularly attractive with its curved side panels. The settle has very early origins, dating back as far as the twelfth century, and later versions often had drawers or cupboard space under the seat. This example has two hinged cupboard doors, and when it is not in use as a seat, the settle can become a useful cabinet with a shelf for books and ornaments.

In common with all such period English furniture, the settle should be made of oak, and as the main requirement is solid oak, the best source is the second-hand and antiques markets, where old pieces of furniture can be broken up to provide the amount needed. Of course, you can also make up your own boards from several lengths of oak, jointed together along their edges with tongues and grooves, in much the same way that the salvaged material would have been joined originally.

You can choose your own dimensions for the settle if you prefer, but the illustrated example is probably best for most households. It is a scaled-down version of the early settle idea, and is both neat and compact.

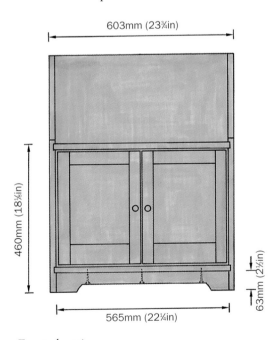

Front elevation.

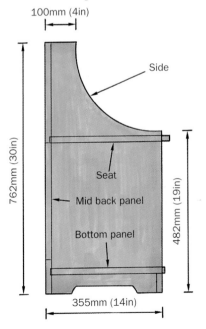

Side elevation.

The finished oak settle.

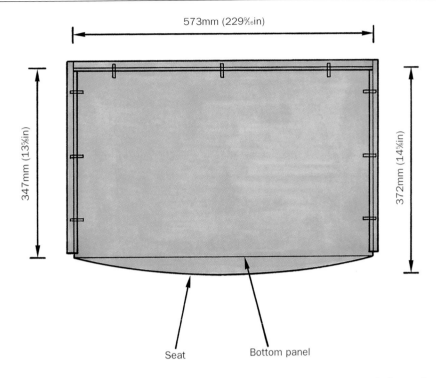

573mm (22⁹⁄₁₆in)

347mm (13⅝in)

372mm (14⅝in)

Plan.

Seat

Bottom panel

The Oak Settle Cutting List

Side:	Two of 762 × 355 × 19mm (30 × 14 × ¾in)
Seat:	One of 575 × 372 × 19mm (22⅝ × 14⅝ × ¾in)
Bottom panel:	One of 575 × 347 × 19mm (22⅝ × 13⅝ × ¾in)
Top back:	One of 575 × 330 × 19mm (22⅝ × 13 × ¾in)
Mid back:	One of 575 × 330 × 19mm (22⅝ × 13 × ¾in)
Bottom back:	One of 575 × 100 × 19mm (22⅝ × 4 × ¾in)
Front valance:	One of 565 × 63 × 19mm (22¼ × 2½ × ¾in)
Narrow door stile:	Three of 355 × 50 × 19mm (14 × 2 × ¾in)
Wide door stile:	One of 355 × 56 × 19mm (14 × 2¼ × ¾in)
Top door rail	Two of 255 × 50 × 19mm (10 × 2 × ¾in)
Bottom door rail:	Two of 255 × 63 × 19mm (10 × 2½ × ¾in)
Door panel:	Two of 255 × 192 × 4mm (10 × 7⁹⁄₁₆ × ³⁄₁₆in)

If the acquisition of the oak boards has entailed the breaking up of an old wardrobe, cabinet or a few unwanted bed-ends, one of the first tasks is to remove any old surface treatment, such as stain and varnish. This work can often be carried out by an obliging local joinery, which will have machinery to skim a thin layer off both faces, or you can do the preparation yourself with a smoothing plane or electric plane, finishing off by rubbing down thoroughly with sandpaper.

Begin by making a card template for the two side members. The curve is drawn to a diameter of 230mm (9in) using a makeshift compass, which consists of a length of 25 × 13mm (1 × ½in) wooden batten that has a hole drilled at one end for a pencil and a panel pin at the other end. Cut out the template with a sharp knife and draw the outline of the side onto two 19mm (¾in) thick oak boards. In marking out the boards, decide which surface is to appear on the outside of the finished settle, in case there are any minor blemishes or imperfections, which would be better

53

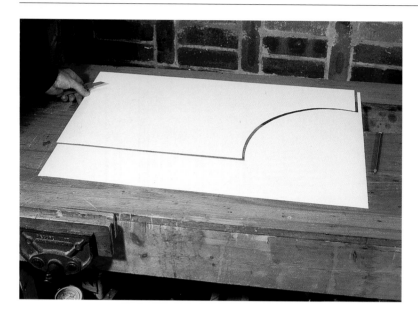

Cutting out the card template for the side-panels.

concealed on the inside, and place the template accordingly.

Mark in the positions of the housing joint grooves for the seat and the bottom panel, which must match precisely the thickness of the boards used for these two parts. It is possible to cut the grooves with the saw and chop out the waste with a chisel and mallet, but the best result will be obtained using an electric router.

As it is almost impossible to fit a cutter into the router that matches exactly the required width of the groove – which may be slightly more or less than 19mm (¾in) – the best method is to use a 6mm (¼in) straight cutter and make up to three cuts across the side-members for each groove. The path of the router is guided by clamping a length of straight-edged batten across the width of the side member so that the router always cuts within the marked area. Set the depth of the cutter to 4mm (³⁄₁₆in), and finally clean up the groove with a chisel to remove loose strands of oak.

Repeat this procedure until all four housing grooves have been cut, then mark in and cut the rebates for the back panel, to the same depth of 4mm (³⁄₁₆in). Unlike the housing grooves for the

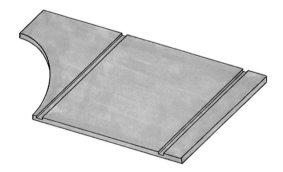

The housing joint grooves for the seat and bottom-panel.

seat and bottom panel, which are cut at right-angles to the grain of the wood, the rebates are cut in the same direction as the grain, along the rear edge of both side members. However, as the two side members are still only marked out on the oak boards and not yet cut to size, the rebate for the back panel is cut as just another groove, and requires the use of the long straight-edged batten to align the router.

Now cut out the side members using a jigsaw, working it carefully around the curved lines. Any slight irregularities in the cut can be smoothed out with the spokeshave, and by gently rubbing with sandpaper, checking that both curves maintain the same appearance. Plane the front and rear edges straight and square.

A portion of waste is removed from the bottom edge of both sides to leave two short foot projections. Each foot is 63mm (2½in) wide at the bottom, where the settle will come into contact with the ground, and the waste is cut to a depth of 25mm (1in). Once again, curves should be drawn in to an equal degree, back and front, and the unwanted portion of wood cut away with the jigsaw.

Next, cut the three back panels to size. Two of these are 330mm (13in) wide, and the third is 100mm (4in). They are attached together, edge to edge, to form one continuous panel, the best joint for this purpose being the tongue-and-groove. In this instance, the tongue is a strip of hardwood, which slots into two grooves cut in adjoining edges.

Begin by cutting each of the three back-panel components to a length of 573mm (22⅞in), and then plane all the edges square so that the three panels butt up against one another without leaving any gaps. Take the topmost of these and cut a groove along its lower edge with the router fitted with a 4mm (³⁄₁₆in) cutter. Set in the groove by 4mm (³⁄₁₆in) from the rear face of the board and cut to a depth of 6–9mm (¼–⅜in). If your tool-box contains a plough plane, this could be used instead to cut the grooves.

Repeat the same procedure for the upper and lower edges of the middle panel, and the upper edge of the narrow bottom panel, so that the grooves are all cut in corresponding positions. Cut two tongues from strips of hardwood measuring 573mm (22⅞in) in length and 13 × 4mm (½ × ³⁄₁₆in) in cross-section and tap each of these into their grooves until the joints are fully located and the three panels fit tightly up against one another. Do not attempt to glue the joints together yet.

Fit the back panel temporarily into place within the rebates of the two side members, and mark in the positions of the seat and the bottom panel at both ends, so that you can tell where the housing grooves need to be cut. Then dismantle the three parts of the back panel, mark in the grooves and cut these with the router, using the same method as before, aligning the router against a clamped piece of straight-edged batten, and cutting to a depth of 4mm (³⁄₁₆in).

Prepare another card template for the seat and the bottom panel, which are identical, other than for the fact that the seat additionally has a gentle curve on its front edge, bowed out by 25mm (1in) at the centre. The template should have the curve included; it may be drawn freehand, unless you prefer the absolute precision of a compass – that is to say, the long length of wood with a pencil inserted through a hole at one end, and a panel pin at the other end to act as a pivot. Either way, transfer the pattern on to two 19mm (¾in) thick oak boards, one to include the curve of the seat, the other with the simple straight edge of the bottom panel, and cut these out with the jigsaw, once again running over the curve with

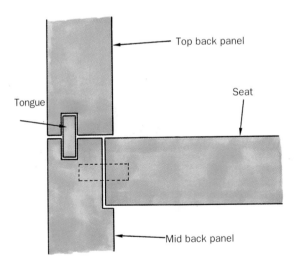

The tongued-and-grooved jointing of the back-panels.

55

the spokeshave, and planing the straight edges square and true. Check that the two panels fit properly into the housing grooves in the side members.

Cut the front valance from a piece of oak measuring 63 × 19mm (2½ × ¾in), noting that this is, in fact, a little shorter than the seat, back and bottom panels, because it does not have its own housing grooves to slot into, but butts up directly against the inside faces of the sides. It is secured to the underside of the bottom panel with three screws, and dowelled to the sides, and has a similar cutaway portion to give a foot at each end, matching those already cut in the sides.

All of the joints are now ready to be measured for the dowels that will be used to secure them in place. The positioning of the dowels is not crucial, as long as they are evenly spaced out and not located too close to the edges; but you must ensure that each dowel hole position is marked precisely between corresponding parts of the joint to guarantee accurate fitting together when the glue is applied.

Drill out the holes to a depth of just over 9mm (⅜in) each, using a 6mm (¼in) diameter auger bit mounted in a handbrace. Cut thirty-six lengths of 6mm (¼in) diameter dowelling, each measuring fractionally under 19mm (¾in) long, and chamfer the ends slightly by giving a couple of twists in a pencil sharpener. Run a

A dowel, with its ends chamfered, ready for use.

hacksaw blade along the length of each dowel to cut a shallow notch for the glue to squeeze out during assembly.

Rub down each of the boards with sandpaper, starting with a medium grade and finishing with fine. Brush away all of the particles of wood dust and apply wood glue to the joints. It is best to commence by assembling the back and fitting the seat and bottom panel into their respective grooves before joining this sub-assembly to one side member. Fit the front valance, then place the other side member in position, line up the dowels with their holes and tap this fully home, using the mallet and a large clean piece of scrap oak to avoid damaging the surface of the side. Turn the assembly over and knock the joints completely together on the other side. Finally, cramp up the settle and wipe away all traces of excess glue from the joints with a damp rag, leaving it for at least a day while the glue sets hard.

Complete the assembly by fixing the front valance to the bottom panel with three 50mm (2in) No. 8 woodscrews.

The next step is to make the two doors. These are framed and panelled doors, and, if you have already pursued the idea of salvaging oak from old furniture in order to make the settle, the most suitable source of material for the doors is an oak-panelled wardrobe or bed-end because this provides not only the oak-veneered plywood but also the solid oak sections for the door frame, with the groove already cut to receive the panelling.

Starting with the solid oak, plane it thoroughly to remove all the stain and varnish, and cut it to the required lengths and widths. Note that the two upper rails measure 50mm (2in) wide and the two lower rails 63mm (2½in) wide. In the case of the stiles, three of these are cut to a width of 50mm (2in), but the fourth is 56mm (2¼in). The reason for this is that rebates are cut in the two edges where the doors meet, so that when both doors are closed, the two adjacent stiles appear to be equal, when in fact one projects behind the other to act as a stop, as is usual with the closing of two doors.

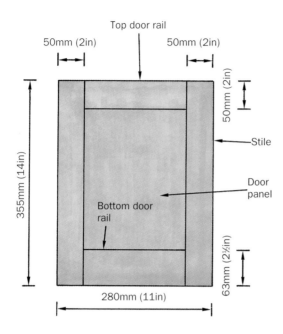

Front elevation of door.

The rails and stiles are assembled with haunched mortise and tenon joints. The purpose of the haunches is to hide the grooves cut in the stiles, which would otherwise show on the top and bottom edges of the doors. The mortises should be cut to a width of 6mm (¼in), equal to the width of the groove, and a depth of 38mm (1½in). The secondary shoulders of the tenons are inset by 9mm (⅜in).

Prepare all of the joints, checking that each fits fully into place to produce two door-frames with right-angled corners, then mark and cut the rebates in the two adjacent door-stiles with the router or the plough plane, cutting each rebate to a depth of 6mm (¼in), and to half the thickness of the material.

Cut the two door-panels from the sheet of oak-veneered plywood, allowing at least 6mm (¼in) extra to fit into each groove. Clean off any stain or varnish from the two veneer faces, and assemble the joints with wood glue. Do not apply glue to the panels, as these are left free inside their grooves.

The plywood door-panel is scraped clean with the chisel, one of the door stiles already having been planed to size.

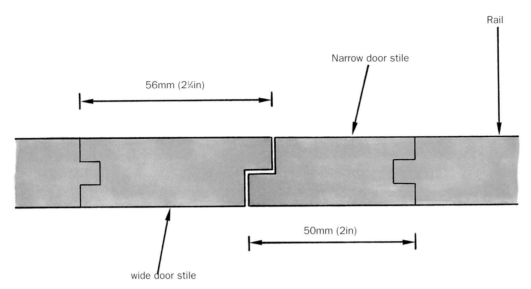

Plan of door-stile rebates.

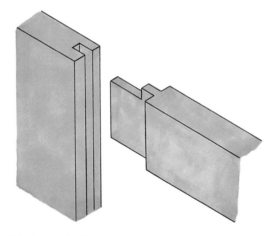

The haunched tenon.

Fit two 63mm (2½in) solid brass butt hinges to each door, rebating as necessary, and then mark the hinge positions on the insides of the settle. Fit round oak door-knobs, which can be purchased at most woodcraft shops; to avoid their fixing screws from being seen on the insides of the doors, cover them with small shiny steel furniture glides, which simply tap into place. The doors may be kept shut with small furniture bolts and catches.

Various types of finish are possible for the settle. The illustrated example was given two applications of dark oak-wood stain, followed by wax polish rubbed thoroughly into the wood and repeated several times.

CHAPTER 8

The Child's High Chair

Most babies' high chairs have developed into folding, lightweight, easy-to-clean seats with detachable plastic trays, and these serve a very useful purpose when the child is small and still needs to be strapped in. But what happens once the child has outgrown the baby chair? Most parents simply sit their children at the table in an ordinary chair, and let them get used to reaching up to the table until they grow big enough to sit comfortably.

Our child's high chair is an in-between seat. It is not equipped with a food tray or harness, but it is high off the ground, has armrests to prevent the child from falling off the seat, and the four legs are splayed outwards for stability. You could make the chair from any wood you

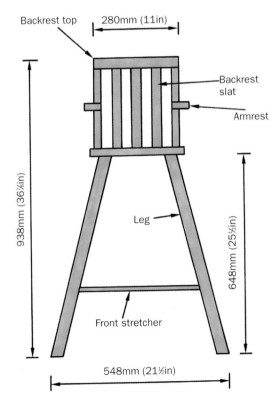

Front elevation.

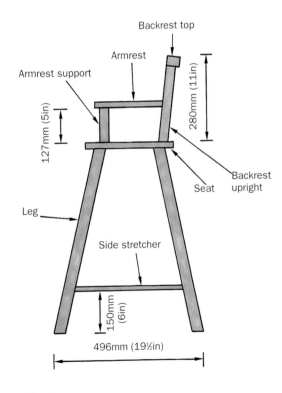

Side elevation.

59

The finished high chair.

The Child's High Chair Cutting List

Seat:	One of 305 × 305 × 19mm (12 × 12 × ¾in)
Leg:	Four of 673 × 45 × 45mm (26½ × 1¾ × 1¾in)
Armrest:	Two of 242 × 50 × 19mm (9½ × 2 × ¾in)
Armrest support:	Two of 134 × 32 × 19mm (5⅜ × 1¼ × ¾in)
Backrest upright:	Two of 267 × 32 × 19mm (10½ × 1¼ × ¾in)
Backrest top:	One of 280 × 38 × 38mm (11 × 1½ × 1½in)
Backrest slat:	Three of 254 × 32 × 9mm (10 × 1¼ × ⅜in)
Front stretcher:	One of 432 × 16mm (17 × ⅝in)
Back stretcher:	One of 432 × 16mm (17 × ⅝in)
Side stretcher:	Two of 388 × 16mm (15¼ × ⅝in)

choose, but this example is built from pine. It will be painted anyway, for a glossy surface enables you to clean it easily – children have a remarkable habit of getting their food everywhere – and a bright colourful chair is more suitable than one that is stained and varnished, although this is a good alternative if you want to match the chair up with other pine furniture.

Unlike a conventional chair, where the backrest is a continuation of the back leg and is made from the same piece of wood, this chair is made in two parts: the seatback and the armrests are jointed to the upper surface of the seat, making for a rigid structure; and the legs are jointed separately underneath.

The first step is to make the seat, since everything else attaches to it. As in other instances where you want to make a solid board, this is made up of smaller boards joined together. The seat measures 305 × 305mm (12 × 12in), and the easiest method is to join tongued-and-grooved boards of the sort that are supplied as floorboard material. This does, of course, restrict you to using white wood or

redwood, otherwise you will have to prepare your own tongues and grooves, but as it has been decided to make this particular chair from pine, the knotty floorboards are quite acceptable. The boards are quoted as being 150 × 25mm (6 × 1in), but in fact they measure 140 × 19mm (5½ × ¾in) including the tongue. Take three lengths of board, each measuring slightly more than the required 305mm (12in), and apply glue to their tongues and grooves, pushing the joints firmly together. Lay the assembly on a single sheet of newspaper lying on the flat surface of the workbench, wipe away excess glue and leave for a day to set hard.

Peel off the newspaper – it may have stuck to some of the surplus glue – and rub down both surfaces thoroughly with sandpaper. This will enable you to judge which is the better surface to face uppermost. At this stage, the board will be longer and wider than required, so the excess amounts must be trimmed away. One edge will still have a tongue and the other has a groove. In reducing the board to 305mm (12in) wide, take equal amounts from both sides, cutting away the waste with the jigsaw or handsaw, and planing the edges square and smooth. To bring the seat to its correct length of 305mm (12in), square a straight line across both ends, but as this now entails cutting across the grain, mark along the pencil line with a sharp knife so that when you follow up with the saw, the saw-blade does not lift the grain but makes a clean cut instead.

Round off the four corners to remove the pointedness, which could be harmful to the child. This needs no more than a rub down with coarse sandpaper, although you could pencil in the curves to make certain that they are all the same. Round off the four upper edges as well. It is possible that a closer inspection of the seat may reveal some degree of curvature, either from the way the tongues and grooves butted up against each other, or because the wood itself was inherently curved. Ordinarily, this could prove quite troublesome but in this case it does not really matter, since

Sawing the seat to size.

you would merely arrange for the concave, bowed-in surface to face uppermost. Some seats are shaped like this anyway.

The next step is to cut the four legs to length from 45 × 45mm (1¾ × 1¾in) material. This is rather a large section of wood and might be associated more with a full-sized chair for an adult. However, its more substantial size is preferred for this chair because it lowers the centre of gravity, which, combined with the angle of splay, makes for greater stability. Bearing in mind that children like to tilt their chairs back if they can, you cannot afford to have a chair that topples easily, and this one does not. Each leg should be measured to 660mm (26in) plus an additional 13mm (½in) for the tenon.

The hardest part of making this chair is to get the angles right for the joints between the legs and the seat. Normally, a tenon fits straight into a mortise in line with the leg but each leg is sloped out in two dimensions: to the side, and to the back or the front. This makes for a complex tenon.

However, the mortises come first and these are straightforward. Measure and mark their positions in the usual way: set the spurs of the mortise gauge to a gap of 19mm (¾in) and adjust the fence of the gauge so that the two

parallel lines are 38mm (1½in) from the side of the seat, and stop 32mm (1¼in) from the front or back edge, depending on which leg the mortise is for. The mortise length is 38mm (1½in). Drill and chop out the waste from each mortise to a depth of 13mm (½in), taking care not to cut right through the thickness of the seat.

As the legs are sloped outwards, the only realistic way of preparing four equal tenons is to make a template from which each tenon can be marked. You will appreciate the angle that the legs form when you realize that the distance between the legs where they join the seat is approximately 170mm (6¹¹⁄₁₆in), whereas at ground level the distance is 458mm (18in) between each of the front legs and back legs, and 406mm (16in), from front to back. The point is, these amounts are not absolutely critical; what really matters is that they should serve as a guide from which you can prepare the template, which is used for all the legs. The top of each leg, where the tenon is cut, is a complicated shape and the template needs careful preparation, for no part of the tenon can be marked in the normal way with the mortise gauge, even though it must be 19mm (¾in) wide to match the mortise. A further point to bear in mind is that when you have prepared the paper or card template, it has to be applied to the top of each leg in opposite directions for both pairs of front and back legs, as they are sloped in different directions. Mark each tenon in pencil and cut away the waste with the tenon saw, cleaning up with the chisel. Make a trial fitting to ensure that all four joints are perfect.

The legs are held in place with 19mm (¾in) diameter dowelling stretcher rails. The front and back stretchers are set 228mm (9in) up from the bottom of the legs, and the side stretchers are set 150mm (6in) up likewise. Each dowel hole should be drilled to a depth of 25mm (1in) and, once again, the drill-bit cannot simply bore straight into the wood but must be angled to take account of the splay. It is inadvisable to quote a length for each of the stretchers, for there is too much room for error; you must determine the appropriate length according to the geometry of your own seat. Cut to length, fit the joints together, but do not glue them yet. Mark their respective positions with reference numbers or letters, and take them apart again.

The chairback and armrests come next. The chairback is made up of a curved top rail, cut from 38 × 38mm (1½ × 1½in) material, whose overall length is 280mm (11in). At each end is a supporting upright, which measures 242mm (9½in) minus the tenons or 267mm (10½in) overall. Three backrest slats fit between the top rail and the seat, and the whole assembly is raked back. A pair of armrests, fitted with their own vertical supports at the front, are joined to the backrest uprights. All parts are assembled with mortise and tenon joints.

Mark the curvature of the top rail, either freehand or with drawing curves, and prepare to the required shape with the spokeshave, rubbing down afterwards with medium-grade sandpaper to smooth out any unevenness. Cut the two backrest uprights from 32 × 19mm (1¼ × ¾in) material, and mark in a mortise at each end on the underside of the top rail. It will have to be rather a small mortise, otherwise the end of the top rail will split; its width should be 9mm (⅜in), its length no more than 13mm (½in) and its depth the same. Because the two mortises are so close to the ends of the top rail, the material will not withstand a heavy chopping action with the chisel; instead, you should aim to drill out the bulk of the waste, and gently pare away the remainder with a narrow chisel which, if it is well sharpened, will cut easily into the corners of the mortise.

Shaping the top backrest rail with the spokeshave.

Matching tenons can be marked in with the gauge at the top end of the two backrest uprights; you will notice that there is a surplus of wood that juts out beyond the curved edges of the top rail. Cut the tenons and, when these fit perfectly, dismantle temporarily, so that the positions of the three backrest slat mortises can be marked in and cut. The slats are made from 32 × 9mm (1¼ × ⅜in) wood, and they should be arranged at regular intervals between the two uprights, separated by a gap of approximately 34mm (1⅜in) each, with mortises cut on the seat and the underside of the top rail. All six mortises are 6mm (¼in) wide, 25mm (1in) long and cut to a depth of 6mm (¼in). Prepare a matching tenon at both ends of each backrest slat.

Now apply wood glue to the two joints between the backrest uprights and the top rail, and tap these fully home. This is an important first stage because, when the glue has set hard, the jutting-out edges of the uprights must be planed down to bring them into alignment with the curved top rail. The chairback is raked at an angle of 5 degrees, and the tenons are marked at the bottom of each upright.

As the three backrest slats have already had their tenons cut at both ends, any one of these may be used to mark the correct length of the two uprights and the point at which the bottom tenon commences. Mark in both the tenons, set at the required 5-degree angle, and cut away the waste with the tenon saw. Make a test-fitting of the entire chairback assembly, and keep this in position, without glue, whilst the armrests and their front supports are prepared.

Measure and mark the two armrests to size. They are 50mm (2in) wide at the front, tapering in a gentle flowing curve to a width of 19mm (¾in), to match the backrest upright. The armrest supports are both 125mm (5in) in length, minus tenons, and are cut from 32 × 19mm (1¼ × ¾in) material. Mortises need to be cut in the underside of the armrest, set back 19mm (¾in) from the front end, in a corresponding position on the seat, and in the backrest upright, in such a position that the armrest is horizontal. Tenons to match are cut at both ends of each armrest support, and at the back end of the armrest, angled to take account of the sloped chairback.

When all the joints have been cut and tested for an accurate fit, rub down all components thoroughly. This is an important part of the preparation, because all parts of the chair need to have well-rounded edges.

Assemble the chair in two stages. First, glue all the joints for the chairback, the armrests and their supports, tapping all the joints fully home and checking that the correct angles are

Planing the front edge of the uprights, to bring them into alignment with the top backrest rail.

Making a trial assembly of the top backrest rail and uprights into the seat.

The two armrests are placed side by side in the vice and their curves shaped with the spokeshave.

Assembling the seat.

maintained between the chairback and the seat, and the armrests where they join the chairback, and clean away all surplus glue. When this has set firmly, apply more wood glue to the tenons at the top of the legs and the receiver holes for the dowelled stretcher rails, and fit these together.

As a finishing touch, trim the bottom of each leg so that it rests flat on the ground, and paint the chair in your desired colour.

Assembling the legs.

The finished joint stool.

CHAPTER 9

The Joint Stool

The joint stool is an interesting piece of furniture that dates from the late-sixteenth and early-seventeenth centuries, undergoing small but somewhat significant changes during that period, mainly with regard to the turning of the legs and the amount of decorative detail on the rails. The seat was invariably a flat rectangular piece of oak, with a simple thumbnail moulding worked on each of its four edges. Being of rudimentary design, all of the joints were pegged with dowels and the seat fastened in place to the tops of the four legs in similar fashion, with larger dowels. The legs, rails and stretchers would all have been made from oak, as, indeed, were the dowels.

Whereas the original purpose of the joint stool would have been to sit at a refectory table, or something of that sort, in our own contemporary world it could be considered not only to be a useful little seat but also, as an alternative purpose, a small occasional table. Modern reproduction-style coffee-tables have much in common with this particular item of early English furniture.

The difference between an Elizabethan and a Jacobean joint stool chiefly being concerned with the amount of decorative detail, and how it is applied, it is a question of individual preference whether the legs should be turned to a fairly plain and conventional pattern, as in this instance, and the rails only given two straight grooves; or whether, more ornately, the legs should be turned and then carved and possibly fluted, and the rails decorated with

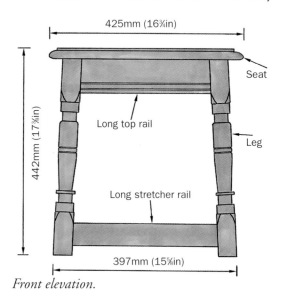

Front elevation.

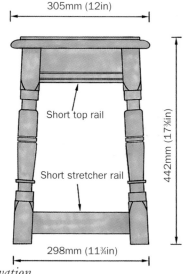

Side elevation.

The Joint Stool Cutting List

Seat:	One of 425 × 305 × 22mm (16¾ × 12 × ⅞in)
Leg:	Four of 420 × 42 × 42mm (16½ × 1⅝ × 1⅝in)
Long top rail:	Two of 323 × 72 × 22mm (12¾ × 2¹³⁄₁₆ × ⅞in)
Short top rail:	Two of 221 × 72 × 22mm (8¾ × 2¹³⁄₁₆ × ⅞in)
Long stretcher rail:	Two of 357 × 48 × 22mm (14 × 1⅞ × ⅞in)
Short stretcher rail:	Two of 257 × 48 × 22mm (10⅛ × 1⅞ × ⅞in)

intricate carvings, such as arcaded curves. The legs may be upright, but usually they are a little splayed out for greater stability.

Unless you intend deliberately copying one particular period in the most rigorous manner, as if it were intended to be an absolute reproduction of a single style, you will probably decide in your own mind how you would like the piece to look when it is finished, combining a variety of characteristics to suit. This is not, of course, the purist's approach, but it will undoubtedly give you the most desirable result. The design for this joint stool has been kept as plain as possible, partly because I did not wish to produce something that was too complicated, and partly because it suited my own idea of how a joint stool ought to look.

Oak is the natural choice for this piece, the legs being turned from 42 × 42mm (1⅝ × 1⅝in) cross-section, the rails from 72 × 22mm (2¹³⁄₁₆ × ⅞in) and the stretchers from 48 × 22mm (1⅞ × ⅞in) material. The seat is a board of solid oak measuring 425mm (16¾in) in length, 305mm (12in) in width and 22mm (⅞in) thick. If you have been able to accumulate a stock of wood derived from old second-hand furniture, the stuff of house clearances, the stool seat can be cut from a conveniently sized panel of solid material; otherwise it will be necessary to join a board together from narrower sections – either

by butt-jointing, dowel-jointing or cutting tongues and grooves. The piece of oak used here was, in fact, salvaged from a bed-end acquired at a reasonable price from a secondhand furniture shop.

The legs are made first. Our design has splayed legs, which makes for a more stable stool; and although the degree of splay is quite small, it does, nevertheless, introduce angles that are greater or less than 90 degrees, depending on which way you look at them. For the moment, however, it is merely enough to measure the legs to length, allowing at least 25mm (1in) extra at each end, later to be trimmed off when joints have been cut and vital stages of assembly completed.

Wood-turning, it must be remembered, is a skill that requires a lot of practice to reach perfection. If this is to be your first attempt at wood-turning, do not be put off the idea, but you would certainly be well-advised to begin on scraps of softwood, graduating to small bits of oak. It does not matter whether you have the use of a full-sized workshop lathe, a miniature low-powered version or, indeed, a lathe accessory driven by an electric drill: each of these will produce first-class results provided you work within the scope of the equipment.

First, mark in the two positions that denote the top and bottom ends of the legs, which will remain as they are, square in cross-section. It is the length in between these that is the section to be turned, and the initial step is to rough this into a cylindrical shape with the spindle gouge. Once the cylinder is smooth and even, this part now has the various positions of its decorative features measured and clearly marked along its length in pencil, making sure that the pencil lines are bold enough to be visible when the wood is spinning at high speed. The diameters of the various segments should be checked often, with calipers or a similar home-made gauge, to ensure that they are turned to the required amount, not too little and not too much. Consistency is very important at this stage, since each of the four legs is to be identical. However, the pattern is straight-

Turning the leg on the lathe.

Marking a top rail mortise on one leg.

forward, without complications, the most difficult part being the turning of the square corners where the extremities of the turned part meets the square top and bottom ends.

Cut the decorative grooves with the parting tool and smooth all of the turned surfaces with abrasive paper, commencing with a fairly coarse grit before finishing off with fine. Beware of the large amount of dust that this will create, and cover your face with a suitable dust-mask.

Having turned the first leg, carry on with the second and then the third and the fourth. Even the most experienced wood-turner will find it difficult to guarantee exactly the same result for all four legs, and it might be necessary to re-mount completed legs in the lathe again to remove a little more here and there until a near-perfect match is obtained. Only a fully automatic machine can provide absolute accuracy, and if there are slight differences, these usually have to be accepted as part of your stool's unique character!

Once the four legs have been turned satisfactorily, mark in the positions of the rail and stretcher mortises on each one. Note that these are not set centrally across the width of the legs' remaining square sections, but placed near to the outside edges. This immediately presents us with an interesting question: which are the outside edges? The matter is quite arbitrary, but it is usual to inspect each leg carefully and choose those two surfaces, in each

instance, which have the least blemishes. The mortise width is 13mm (½in) in each case, set in by 6mm (¼in) from both ends. The rail mortises shall therefore be 60mm (2⅜in) in length and the stretcher mortises 36mm (1⅜in) long. Scribe each mortise 9mm (⅜in) from the outside edges of the legs so that when assembled, the rails and stretchers are effectively set in by 4mm (³⁄₁₆in).

Mount each leg in the workbench vice, and chop out the mortises to a depth of 22mm (⅞in). This does not have to be absolutely accurate, but if you cut any deeper, the mortises will meet inside the wood; if you cut any less, the tenons will consequently be shorter, compromising the strength of each joint – though they will eventually be pegged in place.

Although the legs are to be splayed out from top to bottom, the ends of each mortise may be cut squarely into the wood, for the splay is only slight, and the tenons can be trimmed when the joints are ready to be fitted together before final assembly.

If you wish to decorate the top rails with fluting, this is the best time to do it, before cutting the tenons. Carved work would be better carried out after the jointing has been completed, when the rails are cut to their final length, when carved patterns can be marked accurately on to the wood; but for fluting, which is best accomplished with the router, the task is much easier if the decorative lines are

Chopping out the mortise with a chisel and mallet.

Cutting top rail decorations with the electric router.

applied to a single long piece of wood, before it is cut up into individual rails. A veining cutter is suitable for this type of decoration, run in two parallel lines close to the bottom edge.

Next, prepare to mark the tenons. This is where the splay of the leg is determined, for the stretcher is longer than its corresponding top rail. You may find it helpful to take a large sheet of plain paper and draw a full-sized side and end elevation of the stool in order to give you an accurate guide upon which to place the wood for marking out the tenons; however, this is not strictly necessary. Take a tip – mark and cut the tenons for the rails first, and when they are fitting perfectly, measure and mark the stretchers likewise. You may discover that there is a subtle difference between the drawing and the real thing, caused by several factors: minor inaccuracies in the positioning of the mortises, imperceptible curvature of the wood from which the legs are cut, to name but two. By measuring the stretcher rail when the top rail is in position, the length can be determined with precision.

If you are prepared to rely on measurement only, mark in the tenons according to the following dimensions: the lengths, minus tenons, are 270mm (10⅝in) for the top edge and 278mm (10¹⁵⁄₁₆in) for the bottom edge of the long rails; 306mm (12in) for the top edge and 312mm (12¼in) for the bottom edge of the long stretchers; 168mm (6⅝in) for the top edge

and 176mm (6¹⁵⁄₁₆in) for the bottom edge of the short rails; and 206mm (8⅛in) for the top edge and 212mm (8⅜in) for the bottom edge of the short stretchers. Scribe in the tenon at each end of these pieces with the mortise gauge, set to mark its parallel lines centrally across the thickness of the wood, to a length of 22mm (⅞in), equal to the depth of the mortises. The tenon shoulders will not be squared across, as they usually are, but angled slightly in accordance with the lengths quoted above.

Cut each of the tenons with the tenon saw, carefully removing the waste and trimming the shoulders with the chisel. Make a trial fit in each instance, marking the corresponding mortise and tenon with some form of identification, such as the letters A, B, C, D, etc., so that each joint will be fitted correctly during final assembly. When all of the tenons have been cut, check that the frame fits together perfectly, tapping each joint fully into place, and then trim off the 25mm (1in) of waste from the bottom of the four legs, at which point the frame should stand on a flat surface without rocking back and fore.

If any instability is detected, remedy the matter by checking the fitting of the joints and, if these are satisfactory, consider trimming small amounts from the legs that seem to be too long. Make certain that the frame really is standing on a flat surface first, though!

Once you are satisfied that the frame is ready

Cutting a tenon.

Making a trial-fitting of the mortise and tenon joint.

for assembly, dismantle the joints and mark in the hole positions for the dowel pegs. When a mortise and tenon joint is put together with pegs, it is customary to employ a method known as draw-boring, which simply means that the hole in the tenon is marginally off-set from that drilled through the mortise, so that the peg, when it is driven in, tends to pull the joint more tightly together. The off-setting of the tenon hole is therefore in the direction of its shoulder, and only by 1mm (¹⁄₂₅in) or so. Mark and drill two 6mm (¹⁄₄in) diameter holes for the upper (top rail) mortises, and one 6mm (¹⁄₄in) diameter hole for the lower (stretcher) mortises, making sure that each hole starts from the outside edge, passes through the mortise and bores 3–4mm (¹⁄₈in) into the opposite side. Clean out the mortise each time with the chisel, in order to remove wood that has splintered away with the passage of the drill-bit, then fit the tenons back in place temporarily to mark the hole positions, dismantle each joint again and add the 1mm (¹⁄₂₅in) to off-set towards the shoulder, and drill through the sides of the tenons.

For the assembling of the frame, you will need a total of twenty-four dowels, each measuring 32mm (1¹⁄₄in) in length. Long strips of hardwood dowel material can be purchased from DIY stores, but it is much better to make the dowels individually from matching oak. To begin with, take a piece of strong steel plate

(an old door-hinge is quite useful for this purpose) and drill a 6mm (¹⁄₄in) diameter hole through it (simply enlarging one of the hinge's screw holes). Cut a block of oak, 32mm (1¹⁄₄in) long, and mark out and cut strips 9 × 9mm (⅜ × ⅜in) in cross-section. Trim away the square edges with a chisel to form an octagonal pattern, and chamfer one end by giving a few twists in a large pencil-sharpener. Place the bevelled end in the 6mm (¹⁄₄in) diameter hole in the steel plate, and tap the piece right through with a mallet. As it passes through, the waste is stripped off and a perfect cylindrical dowel should emerge. When all twenty-four dowels have been made, prepare to assemble the frame.

A dry assembly is possible but a glued joint will give additional strength. Apply wood glue to each joint and tap the tenon fully into the mortise, knocking each dowel in as far as it will go. Wipe away any excess glue from the joints. The dowels are slightly overlong, so small amounts will be left protruding, but these should be sawn away and the ends pared flush with the surrounding wood, using a chisel.

To complete the frame, mark the tops of the legs in line with the upper edges of the rails and saw away the waste, gently planing the end-grain smooth and flat. This requires great care, since the action of planing across any end-grain has a tendency to split the wood at the far end: short planing strokes should

71

Making the small oak dowel pegs – the steel plate is a door-hinge with one of its holes enlarged to the required 6mm (¼in) diameter.

Assembling the frame with dowel pegs.

First stage of cutting the thumbnail moulding in the four edges of the seat using the electric router.

Assembling the seat to the frame.

therefore be used. Rub down the frame thoroughly with fine sandpaper, particularly with the aim of removing all faint pencil lines.

The seat is a plain rectangle of solid oak, to which a thumbnail moulding is worked along each of the four edges. The thumbnail moulding is best cut with the electric router, although alternatively it can be shaped entirely by hand. To start with, the router is fitted with a straight rebating cutter and the tool adjusted so that a shallow rebate is cut to a width of 19mm (¾in) from the edge, to a depth of 4mm (³⁄₁₆in). It is preferable to begin by cutting across the grain, meaning the width of the piece,

finishing along the direction of the grain or the length of the wood. The reason is that end-grain is more susceptible to splitting when you reach the far edge of the cut, as with planing, and if any splits occur, these will be removed when you cut along the grain afterwards. Even so, you should always take as much care as possible to avoid splitting the wood.

The rebate is, of course, only the initial stage – next, the curved edge is cut. It is unlikely that you will find a suitable thumbnail-profile cutter, so the answer is to take a standard curved cutter and work it in two or three passes, angling the router differently each time to remove small portions of waste with each pass. You will have to guide the router with a very steady hand, but this is essentially a roughing-out process, for the final shape of the moulding will be derived from thorough sandpapering, observing the convention of commencing across the grain and finishing along it.

The seat of the joint stool is secured to the legs with dowels. This might seem a rather unsightly method, since the ends of the four round pegs will be plainly visible on the top surface of the seat, but this is exactly how it would have been done in the sixteenth century – no attempt at concealment. This time, the dowels must be cut and trimmed entirely by hand, chiselling the curved surface bit by bit to a diameter of 16mm (⅝in). It is a more rough-and-ready method than the making of the smaller dowels, which used the steel plate for a former, but if you drill a 16mm (⅝in) diameter hole through a piece of waste oak, and drive each of the handmade dowels into it with the mallet, this will at least show you where to keep trimming and rubbing down with sandpaper, for where the dowel binds inside the hole, it will develop a shiny surface. Once again, chamfer the end of the dowel that is to be inserted into the hole, as this will give easier entry. Each dowel, when completed, should be

approximately 50mm (2in) long.

Mark the dowel positions on the seat, to coincide with the centre of each leg, and drill right through the seat, taking great care not to damage its upper surface. Drill corresponding holes into the end-grain of the four legs, to a depth of 25mm (1in), then apply wood glue both to the holes in the seat and the holes in the legs, and knock in the dowels. When the glue has dried, trim the end of each dowel until it is flush with the seat, and rub down thoroughly with medium and fine-grade sandpaper.

Apply a dark Jacobean oak wood-stain to all of the stool's surfaces, and when this is completely dry – leave for at least two to three days – give an application of wax polish. The more the wood is wax-polished and buffed with a soft cloth – always polishing and rubbing in the direction of the grain – the more the joint stool will take on a satisfying shine; but remember that a genuinely old piece of furniture has taken hundreds of years to attain its patina, so it is impossible to produce the same effect in a matter of days or weeks. Nevertheless, after a few good polishes, the joint stool gives a very convincing appearance of being old!

The finished director's chair.

CHAPTER 10

The Director's Chair

There is nothing very remarkable about this simple folding canvas-covered chair, except that at some time in the past it became associated with the movie business, and has ever since been known as the director's chair. When you sit in one of these modest but comfortable seats, you know you have something in common with all the big screen names of the past, relaxing between scenes on some faraway location. Indoors or out, this is a neat chair that is easy to make and, unlike some of the cinematic marvels that have been created in its midst, does not require a huge budget.

A hardwood should be chosen for this chair, and a medium-priced timber such as sapele or utile is a good choice, one advantage being that both of these materials will produce a fine natural-looking result, if a stained wood-finish is preferred to paint.

The chair is made in three parts, comprising two rigid sides and a collapsible stool that forms the centre piece, hinged to the bottom of each upright leg. As both sides are identical, the method of construction is the same.

Each side is made up of two legs, an armrest, backrest and lower rail, and the space between the armrest and lower rail is occupied by three vertical dowel rails, which serve as decoration.

Measure and mark two lengths of 35 × 22mm (1⅜ × ⅞in) material for the legs, allowing extra at one end for the tenon that will eventually fit into the armrest. Measure accurately the position of the lower rail on each leg, and mark in the mortise. A mortise width

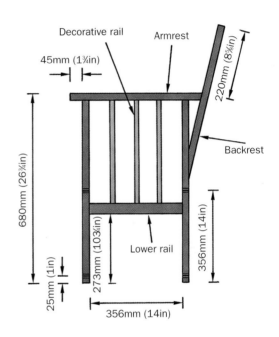

Side elevation.

of 13mm (½in) is appropriate in this instance, being one-third the width of the wood in which it is being cut. Set the spurs of the mortise gauge to this amount, and score two parallel lines along the centre of the marked rail position. Since all of the tenons will be cut with secondary shoulders, the mortise needs to be set in by 3mm (⅛in) at each end. The depth of the mortise should be 16mm (⅝in).

Drill out most of the waste with a 9mm (⅜in) diameter auger-bit mounted in the pillar drill or handbrace, whichever is the more convenient, and chop out the remainder with a 13mm (½in)

The Director's Chair Cutting List

Leg:	Four of 676 × 35 × 22mm (26⅝ × 1⅜ × ⅞in)
Backrest:	Two of 533 × 35 × 22mm (21 × 1⅜ × ⅞in)
Armrest:	Two of 492 × 45 × 22mm (19⅜ × 1¾ × ⅞in)
Lower rail:	Two of 388 × 32 × 22mm (15¼ × 1¼ × ⅞in)
Decorative chair rail:	Six of 373 × 16mm (14¹¹⁄₁₆ × ⅝in)
Stool leg:	Four of 632 × 32 × 16mm (24⅞ x 1¼ × ⅝in)
Seat cross-piece:	Two of 432 × 35 × 25mm (17 × 1⅜ × 1in)
Long stool crossbar:	One of 352 × 16mm (13⅞ × ⅝in)
Short stool crossbar:	One of 312 × 16mm (12¼ × ⅝in)

chisel. When both legs have had the mortise cut, measure and mark the tenon at each end of the lower rail. Adjust the fence of the mortise gauge so that the spurs are centralized on the 22mm (⅞in) edge, and score in the lines.

Cut away the two main shoulders of the tenon with the tenon saw, and then mark in the 3mm (⅛in) secondary shoulders, sawing these off as well. When complete, knock the tenon gently into the mortise to ensure that it is a good fit, but if there is a tendency for the wood to bind, do not force it, but take it apart again. Examine the cheeks of the tenon, and where they appear to be shiny, this indicates the place where there was resistance. Pare away small slivers of wood with the chisel until a good fit is achieved.

Taking the 45 × 22mm (1¾ × ⅞in) material for the armrest, mark out the two mortises on its underside. With the lower rail in place, the two legs are 356mm (14in) apart, and as they

are to remain parallel, the mortises need to be the same distance apart, with the front leg set back 45mm (1¾in) from the front end of the armrest. Although the width of the armrest is 45mm (1¾in), you should keep to the same mortise width of 13mm (½in), re-adjusting the spurs of the mortise gauge to set the spurs in the middle of the material. Prepare the mortises as previously, to a depth of 16mm (⅝in), then dismantle the legs from the lower rail and mark and cut a tenon at the top of each one, in such a way that the legs measure 660mm (26in) in length minus the tenon.

Fit together temporarily the legs, armrest and lower rail, and measure up for the backrest, which requires a specially angled mortise, with the tenon similarly angled. You will also need to measure and cut a wedge from the bottom of the backrest, where it meets the rear surface of the back leg, but this can only be done when the angled mortise and tenon joint has been prepared, since the size of the triangular wedge that must be cut away is dependent on the accuracy of the joint. With the wedge removed, the backrest can be tapped into position, and the side is almost complete.

A nice neat finishing touch is to fit three lengths of 16mm (⅝in) diameter dowelling between the armrest and the lower rail, spaced

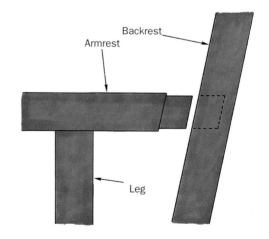

The specially angled mortise joining the back of the armrest to the backrest.

at equal intervals and secured in place by drilling 16mm (⅝in) diameter receiver holes to a depth of 9mm (⅜in) each.

When one side is completed, exactly the same method is employed to make the second, paying particular attention to the backrest, so that it fits at the same angle. At this stage, the various parts are loosely fixed together for convenience. Do not attempt yet to make the fixture permanent.

The stool comes next. It is made in two parts, with a difference in the positioning of the legs – one pair being set inside the other – to permit both halves to be hinged. Taking the outer pair of legs first, measure and mark in the mortise positions on the underside of the seat cross-piece, noting that on this occasion each mortise should be 19mm (¾in) wide to compensate for a reduced length, since the legs are only 16mm (⅝in) thick. The outer legs are set 320mm (12⅝in) apart. Chop out the mortises, and cut matching tenons in the top of the legs. Drill out a 16mm (⅝in) diameter hole through the thickness of each leg, 197mm (7¾in) from the bottom end, to receive a dowel crossbar. When drilling these two holes, do not attempt to bore through in one go, for as the drill-bit emerges on the opposite surface of the wood, it can easily tear away some of the grain.

The three holes cut in the bottom rail to receive the decorative dowel rails.

A better method is to drill through with a 16mm (⅝in) diameter auger or centre bit until the pointed tip of the bit just breaks through the undersurface, then turn the piece over and complete the drilling from the other side. Once again, you can either use the pillar drill or the handbrace.

Repeat this procedure for the second half of the stool, setting the mortises in their complementary position on the cross-piece, where the legs this time are set 280mm (11in) apart.

The next step is to drill rivet holes in each of the upright legs and in each stool leg, copying the pattern of holes in the diagram. Use a 4mm (³⁄₁₆in) twist drill mounted in the pillar drill, which ensures the accuracy and precision necessary for the chair to fold properly once it has been assembled.

Round off the front end of each armrest and the top of each backrest, marking in a suitable semi-circular curve, either with a pair of geometrical compasses or some suitably sized circular object, such as the lid of a jar. Trim off the waste with the jigsaw, completing the curve with the spokeshave and sandpaper.

Plane the long edges of all four legs, the armrests, backrests, the lower seat rails and the stool cross-pieces, rounding them off with a rasp or file, and sandpapering to a smooth finish. The four stool legs are left with square edges.

The chair is now ready for assembly. The joints should be glued and screwed for

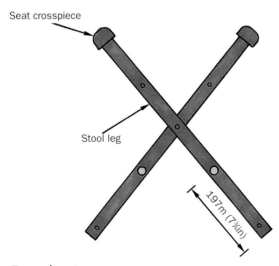

Seat crosspiece

Stool leg

197m (7¾in)

Front elevation.

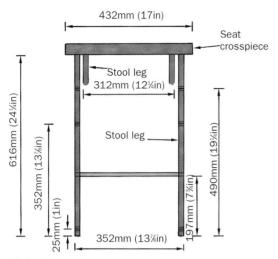

Side elevation.

Making the curved front of the armrest: an alternative to cutting with the jigsaw is to make a series of cuts with the tenon saw.

maximum strength, using a waterproof wood glue and 25 × 2mm (1 × ³⁄₃₂in) mild steel woodscrews. Decide which side is to be on the left and which is to be on the right of the finished chair, and mark the positions of the screws so that they will only be visible on the inside of the chair, leaving the outside surfaces perfect. Drill through the mortise and tenon separately, using a 2mm (³⁄₃₂in) diameter twist drill mounted in a small hand-drill, setting the tenon hole slightly closer to the shoulder of the joint for the technique called draw-boring, so that when the joint is glued and fitted together, the insertion of the screw will pull the tenon more tightly into the mortise. Cover the head of each screw with wood-filler if you intend painting the chair afterwards.

The three parts of the chair are hinged together with rivets made from 4mm (³⁄₁₆in) nails measuring 100mm (4in) in length. Each nail is flat-headed and is converted into a rivet by hacksawing the pointed end off in the appropriate place and tapping around the sawn end with a hard masonry drill and a hammer to squash it out, taking care to avoid denting the wood. Plain washers and a large hard rubber washer are slipped into their respective places

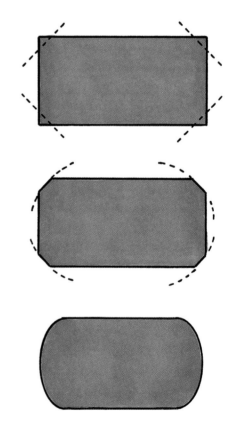

Edge preparation.

to provide a free-moving pivot.

Start the final assembling of the chair by hinging the stool, and then attach it to the four main legs, placing wooden spacer blocks in position on the right-hand side to take up the two gaps. These can be made out of left-over scraps of wood, and each block should measure 28mm (1⅛in) in diameter and 22mm (⅞in) in length, with a 4mm (³⁄₁₆in) diameter hole bored through the centre. Careful drilling, sawing and filing will produce the desired effect.

The four metal brackets come next. Follow the illustrated pattern, using any suitable metal strips of the correct thickness – not less than 2mm (³⁄₃₂in) – that you can find. For instance, the illustrated chair had its brackets made from the salvaged handle of a squeezy kitchen floor mop. So improvise!

Pattern of rivet for hinges.

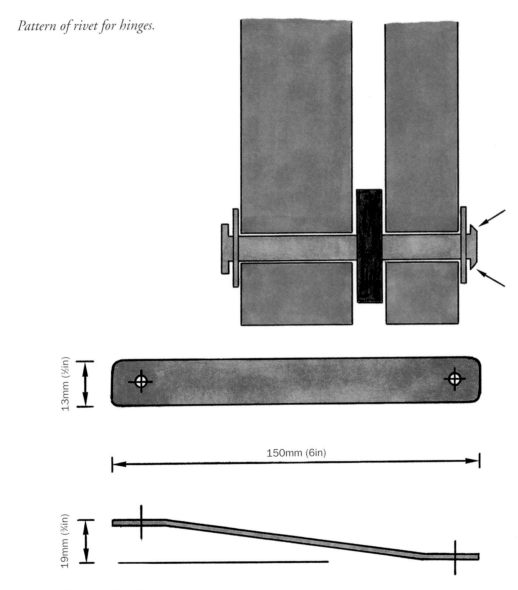

13mm (½in)

150mm (6in)

19mm (¾in)

Pattern for metal brackets.

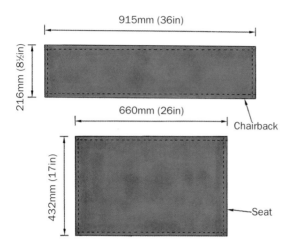

Pattern for seat and chairback fabric.

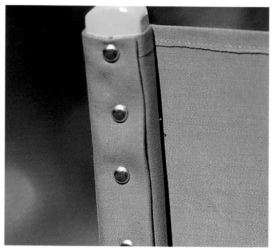

The attachment of the chairback to backrest with brass tacks.

It is recommended that you decide yourself how far apart the holes should be drilled in the metal, referring to the quoted dimensions for guidance only. This is because, due to small variations and errors in individual woodwork, you may find that the dimensions in the text are not precisely right for your own chair. The idea is that when fitted, the brackets should allow the chair to fold up easily, and when unfolded, the stool should not come into contact with the sides but there ought to be a gap of 6mm (¼in).

The brackets are also fixed with rivets. When these are complete, fit the two dowels into the stool legs to act as crossbars, gluing in place. The chair framework is now complete, except for a wood stain, varnish or paint finish.

The material for the seat and back is canvas. Many fabric shops stock a variety of colourful plain and striped materials. Cut to the sizes shown, stitch a 13mm (½in) hem all around and tack into position with round-headed brass furniture tacks. Production is now at an end, and you will find that this chair has its uses everywhere in the house, as well as the garden and, when you fold it up, it can go anywhere you like.

CHAPTER 11

The Deck Chair

You do not have to go on a world cruise to appreciate the lazy comfort of a deck chair. This example has the additional advantage of arms, a leg-rest and canopy to ensure maximum ease. The frame is built of hardwood and the bright, striped fabric is an acrylic fibre. The deck chair uses the same type of joint as the folding chair in the previous chapter, except in lesser numbers, and is simpler and quicker to make.

As usual, the job begins by selecting a suitable hardwood. The choice in this case is iroko, which is very strong and durable, and just right for the long lengths needed for the main framework of the chair, but tends to blunt

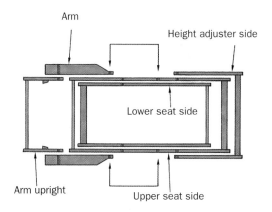

Plan of deck chair.

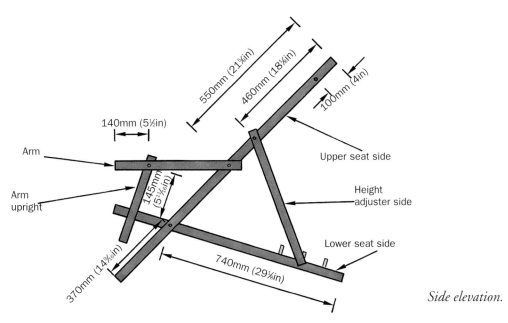

Side elevation.

81

The finished deck chair.

Cutting the back leg to shape with a handsaw.

Marking the decorative rounding at top of the back leg.

Sandpapering the curved surface.

of shallow shoulders. The alternative would be to scribe a circular line with a pair of geometrical compasses. Cut carefully around the marked line with the jigsaw or coping saw to remove most of the waste, and finish off with the spokeshave and chisel, rubbing down with sandpaper, taking care to follow the contour of the curve.

The rounded end of the two armrests should be similarly marked and cut, except that on this occasion 15mm (⅝in) is removed from the 45mm (1¾in) thickness along its length, up to the round front. Once again, the handsaw will probably give the surest cut; finish off by planing the surface with the spokeshave. The armrests need to be cut longer than required,

so that there is sufficient available for the marking and cutting of the tenon that fits into the back leg.

Measure and mark the two front legs to length, again allowing extra for the tenon that will eventually be cut at the top of each one.

The next step is to mark in and cut all of the mortise and tenon joints, which, for the main part of the seat frame, are of the pegged variety. Synthetic waterproof wood glues are well-suited to furniture that may be used out of doors, so there is not the same need for pegs as there was in the past, but they remain a useful assistance during assembly by pulling the tenon firmly into the mortise – the process known as draw-boring.

Rounding off the front of the armrest with the spokeshave.

All the mortises used for jointing the main parts of the frame should be as large as possible, to give maximum strength. It is usual to arrange for the mortise to equal one-third the thickness of the pieces to be joined together, but in this case some of the pieces are of different thickness. For example, all the rails are narrower than the legs; only the armrest is the same. This does not matter greatly, and the most appropriate width for all of the major mortises is 19mm (¾in). Set the spurs of the mortise gauge to this width, and adjust the fence of the gauge so that they mark at the centre of the legs.

Now measure in the positions of the four seat rails and the two lower side rails on all four legs, marking them with a pencil and square. The length of each mortise is determined by the 45mm (1¾in) width of the rails minus 6mm (¼in) at either end where the tenons have secondary shoulders cut. Thus, having set the limits of the mortise, which should be 32mm (1¼in) in length, scribe two parallel lines with the mortise gauge. As the seat rail mortises are each set at exactly the same height in all four legs, when the mortises are cut, they will meet inside the wood. Also mark in the mortise positions for the two backrest rails on the upper part of the two back legs.

The quickest way of removing the waste from the mortise is to drill a series of holes along its length using a drill-bit that is smaller in diameter than the width of the finished joint. Once again, the best tool for the job is the pillar drill fitted with a 16mm (⅝in) diameter wood-drilling bit, its depth guide set to 32mm (1¼in). The handbrace could just as easily be used for this task, only it will be slower and require more effort.

Having bored out the holes, chop out the remaining waste with a 19mm (¾in) chisel and mallet, cutting to the required depth of 32mm (1¼in), and working the chisel carefully to ensure that the sides and ends of the mortise are vertical. Where two adjoining mortises meet inside the wood, as for all four seat rails, their sides should coincide at right-angles and the ends merge without there being any ridges between them, calling for some skill with the chisel.

Now for the rail tenons. Taking each side one at a time, begin by measuring and marking the side seat rails and lower seat rails to length, squaring off at the shoulder positions with pencil lines. Each rail measures 470mm (18½in) overall, or 405mm (16in) minus the tenons. Begin by cutting the rail to length, including the amount needed for the tenons, then, adjusting the mortise gauge fence to scribe its parallel lines centrally across the 32mm (1¼in) thick edge, mark the tenon at each end. Holding the piece in the vice, remove the waste with the tenon saw to form the two shoulders.

Inset the top and bottom edges of the tenon by 6mm (¼in), to match the length of the mortise, and cut away these secondary shoulders. When complete, make a trial assembly of the joint to check that it fits fully home without binding. If there is any tendency to do so, trim the mortise or the tenon until the two parts fit perfectly.

The front and back seat rails come next, together with the two backrest rails. These are identical in length, but just how long they should be is a matter of opinion, for you have the choice of creating a chair whose width suits your own taste, whether it should be wide or narrow. The only point to emphasize is that the chair is designed as a single-seater, so do not be tempted to increase its width to accommodate two or three people, for the seat rails and slats will not be strong enough to take the weight. You would need to increase the size of both, and add a middle seat rail running from front to back.

In this instance, the rails measure 522mm (20½in) overall, or 457mm (18in) minus the tenons. Repeat the same process to mark and cut each tenon, noting that at this stage it is not possible to assemble all of the seat rails into their mortises at the same time, because each tenon blocks the full entry of its partner. The solution is to mark and cut mitres at the end of each pair, so they all fit fully into place.

Loosely assemble both end-frames, consisting of the front and back leg, the side seat rail and the lower side rail, and lay the armrest in position according to its desired height. Once again, you can either copy the plan exactly or alter its position slightly to suit your own preference, but whatever else you do, make certain that you treat both armrests the same. It is best to keep the armrest horizontal and mark in the angle where it meets the sloped back leg. It should be possible to pencil in all the necessary reference marks on the top of the front leg where it meets the underside of the armrest, and the back of the armrest where it meets the back leg, so that the mortise and tenon positions can be marked in at the same time. However, double-check their positions before you cut any of the joints, to ensure that you have not made an error anywhere.

When you are satisfied that all the main

A draw-bored mortise and tenon joint is ready for assembly.

framework joints fit perfectly, prepare to assemble the two end-frames. With all the joints disassembled, mark in the position of each peg-hole, which should be of 6mm (¼in) diameter. Start by measuring and drilling all the holes that pass through the mortises. These are marked on the outward-facing parts of the legs and armrests, and are set in by 9mm (⅜in) from the edge adjacent to the mortise, and placed so that they each pass centrally through the side of it.

Clamp each piece in the vice and drill vertically down through the mortise with a 6mm (¼in) auger in such a way that the drill-bit breaks through on one side of the mortise and crosses its width before boring further into the other side. The hole should be drilled to a total

Assembling a side-member.

depth of 38mm (1½in). Having completed the mortise holes, fit the appropriate tenon fully into position and pass a pencil down the hole – one that just fits in – to mark the centre of the hole on one cheek of the tenon. Dismantle the joint again and adjust the centre of the tenon hole from the pin-point pencil mark, so that it is 2mm (³⁄₃₂in) nearer to the shoulder. Bore this through with the drill and then cut wooden pegs from 6mm (¼in) diameter dowelling, preparing each peg to a length of 50mm (2in). Chamfer one end by giving a few twists in a pencil sharpener – without this, the peg will be unable to fulfil its function.

Apply wood glue to the mortise and tenon joints of all the component parts of one end-frame, tapping the joints firmly together with the mallet and a block of clean scrap wood. Glue the peg-holes and drive each peg into place, leaving 13mm (½in) projecting clear of the surface. Repeat the same procedure for the other end-frame, wiping away any excess glue from around the joints with a damp rag, and leaving the two assemblies for at least a day while the glue sets hard. Trim off the ends of the dowel pegs with a sharp chisel so that they are flush with the surrounding wood, and finish off with sandpaper.

When both end-frames are complete, place the front and back seat rails and the two backrest rails in position, without glue, knocking the joints fully home to check that the seat is perfectly square.

Prepare to fit the five backrest slats. First, measure the distance between the upper and lower backrest rails. Never mind what they ought to be according to the plan, or what you think they ought to be, rely only on the actual measurement, as this will take account of any small errors in the preparation of the joints. One end may be fractionally greater or less than the other. Note all of this down, so that the slats can be cut precisely to the right length. These are likewise fitted with mortise and tenon joints, each slat being prepared from 45 × 19mm (1¾ × ¾in) material.

Mark the lower edge of the upper backrest

Making a trial assembly of the backrest rails and slats.

rail, and the upper edge of its lower partner, arranging the slats at regular intervals. In the illustrated example, they are spaced 38mm (1½in) apart, but this needs to be checked; and the mortises are 13mm (½in) wide, 32mm (1¼in) long and 13mm (½in) deep. They are cut as previously, with the matching tenons measured and marked at both ends of each slat. Make the customary trial assembly to check the soundness and accuracy of all the joints, and then repeat the marking and drilling of the draw-boring holes in the legs, the seat rails and the backrest rails, prepare more dowel pegs and assemble with wood glue, as before.

When the assembly is complete, and the glue has dried, measure and cut five seat slats to a length of 546mm (21½in) from 45 × 19mm (1¾ × ¾in) material with a sixth slat cut so that it fits on top of the front seat rail between the two front legs. The slats should be spaced evenly apart and glued to the tops of the rails. However, each joint should be reinforced with dowel pegs once the glue has dried, the 6mm (¼in) diameter holes being bored at a slight angle, so that the drill can clear the armrest. Cut twelve 50mm (2in) lengths of dowelling and glue these into their holes.

The chair is now finished, apart from requiring a suitable wood treatment to be applied to its surfaces. There are many exterior wood finishes available in a range of natural colours, and the choice is entirely your own. Two coats will give good protection, but this will need to be repeated periodically if the chair is kept outdoors.

The finished coffee-table chair.

together, checking that each one slots fully home and that the four corners form perfect right-angles. Cut the joints for the second side section in the same manner. Before gluing the joints together, place the two assemblies side by side, seat grooves facing inwards, to make sure that they are identical.

Assemble each side section one at a time with wood glue, brushing the glue well into all of the joints and tapping them together with the mallet and a protective block of wood. Cramp up the side assembly, wiping away any excess glue from the joints with a damp rag. When both sides are complete and the glue has set, remove the cramps and rub down the surfaces with medium sandpaper, finishing with a fine-grade paper.

The next step is to make the backrest. The procedure here is almost exactly the same as for making the sides and, indeed, you use the same templates, with a slight modification in the marking out. To begin with, the two upright sections of the backrest, those akin to the legs, are obviously of much greater length – in fact, they are each 705mm (27⅜in) long, with an additional 9mm (⅜in) at the bottom for a tenon – but once they taper to a width of 30mm (1³⁄₁₆in), they maintain this for the rest of their length.

The top of the backrest is an inverted base, but it is given an extra 50mm (2in) of depth. It is also shorter, for whereas the leg bases are 380mm (15in) long, this should measure only 343mm (13½in) and, although it can easily be drawn from the same template as the bases, you must adjust it for its lesser length. However, the mortise and tenon joints between the uprights and the backrest top are identical to those joining the legs to the base, and should be marked and cut in the same way.

At the bottom of the backrest, a base section is fitted but this differs from the bases of the

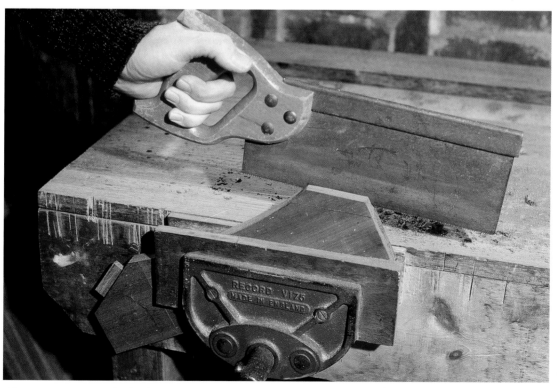

Cutting a tenon in the backrest top.

two sides. It is the same length as the backrest top, although it should be measured and cut overlength to allow for a tenon at either end, and this time both ends are square rather than angled. The curvature is the same as that of the leg bases but needs to be extended before levelling off for the final 30mm (1³⁄₁₆in), where it will form a joint with the uprights. Its maximum width at this point is 60mm (2³⁄₈in).

Prepare the joints between the uprights and the backrest base, which are strictly tongues and grooves, even though they have the same dimensions and method of preparation as the mortise and tenon joints. The mortise, or groove, is cut to a width of 6mm (¼in), a depth of 9mm (³⁄₈in) and is set in 6mm (¼in) from the inside edge of the upright, but continuing to the end of the base, as with a haunch. The tenon, or in this case tongue, is cut at the bottom of the upright, so that it fits into the mortise or groove.

The backrest base is fitted to the bottom inside face of each leg with a conventional mortise and tenon joint, where the mortise, which is cut in the leg, measures 6mm (¼in) in width and 45mm (1³⁄₄in) in length, the four-shouldered tenon being cut at each end of the base.

When the jointing is complete, loosely assemble the backrest to determine the correct positioning of the back seat rail. Standing the three parts of the chair, namely the backrest

First stage of assembly: the back of the chair is joined to one side.

Second stage of assembly: fitting the plywood seat and the front rail.

Third stage of assembly: attaching the second side.

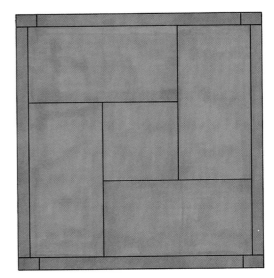

Plan of a woodblock pattern.

and two sides, on a flat surface with their edges abutting, the tenons slotted into their mortises; mark in the position of the back seat rail, so that it is level with the side seat rails. Mark and cut mortise and tenon joints to fit the back seat-rail between the two backrest-uprights, using more grooved material for the rail than was used for the side seat rails. Finally, fit a front seat rail between the inside faces of the legs with mortise and tenon joints, noting that the back rail and front rail, without tenons, measure 283mm (11⅛in) and 343mm (13½in), respectively.

Assemble the backrest with wood glue, so that it becomes a complete sub-assembly like the two sides, cramping it up until the glue has set hard. Once the cramps have been removed, prepare to join the backrest to both sides. The outside edge of each backrest upright is dowel-jointed to the inside of each back leg, using three 9mm (⅜in) dowels equally spaced apart. Since the positioning of these dowels requires great accuracy, use the marking gauge to score a single line along the two outside edges of the backrest assembly, set halfway across its 19mm (¾in) thickness, and then scribe a matching line along the inside face of the two back legs.

Measure and mark the dowel holes in corresponding positions, drilling to a depth of 13mm (½in) in each case. Continue to drill another three equally spaced holes on both outside edges of the uprights from the level of the seat up to the top of the backrest to receive a pair of edge-trims later.

Cut twelve 25mm (1in) lengths of 9mm (⅜in) diameter dowelling, checking that they fit into their receiver holes to the required depth.

The groundwork for the seat is cut from a sheet of 13mm (½in) thick plywood, which should be measured so that it is just large enough to fit into each of the four grooves in the seat rails. Cut it to the required size – approximately 352mm (13⅞in) square – and note that a small rectangular portion will need to be sawn from each of its four corners to enable the panel to fit around those parts of the legs and backrest uprights that have not been grooved.

Make a test-fitting of the chair, slotting the plywood into its grooves, and when you are satisfied that all the joints fit perfectly together, apply wood glue to the seat grooves, the mortise and tenon joints, and the bottom six dowel holes, and assemble the chair around its

103

Assembling the woodblocks.

Fitting edge-trims.

seat, tapping all of the joints fully into place. Wipe surplus glue away from each of the joints, paying particular attention to the seat recess, where the woodblocks are to be fitted for the top of the seat.

Five woodblocks make up the pattern for the seat: four on the outside and one in the middle. These are cut from 9mm (⅜in) thick material, each cut to a width of 113mm (4⅞in). Their exact length can only be determined by the dimensions of the recess, so you must work to your own specifications rather than copying anything quoted here, as it is possible that the overall measurements will differ as a result of small variations in the process of making the chair. The whole point is that when the five wooden blocks are cut to size and fitted into the recess, they should butt tightly up against one another with only a very slight gap showing between them. This needs patience and skill, both in the measuring and the cutting out of each block, but you will appreciate the resulting effect when it is well carried out. Remove the five woodblocks, keeping them in the correct order, and apply wood glue to the recess, brushing it evenly over the plywood and against the inside edges of the seat rails. Place the wooden blocks back into the recess, one at a time, spreading a thin layer of glue over their abutting edges. Press the blocks down firmly, making sure that all trapped air has been squeezed out, and keep the seat under firm pressure for the time it takes for the glue to dry and set hard.

Finish off the chair by making the pair of edge-trims to fit against the upper part of the backrest, each of which copies the curve of the legs, though to a lesser extent, and drill dowel holes to match up with those already drilled in the edges of the backrest uprights. Apply wood glue to the dowels and the joining surfaces, and fit the edge-trims.

Finally, sandpaper thoroughly all the surfaces of the chair, using a fine-grade paper, and complete the chair by rubbing on several applications of teak oil to give the wood a soft lustrous shine.

CHAPTER 14

The Pine Dining-chair

The dining-chair is an important part of the household, for it occupies one of the main rooms in the home and is usually part of a matching set of identical chairs. Its simple, straightforward lines are traditional, with curved back legs and a raked backrest, and the seat, whilst being made of solid wood, avoids plainness by having V-shaped grooves cut across its width, with wedge-shaped edge-pieces running from the front of the seat to the back legs. The seat is fastened to the top edges of the seat rails with glue, strengthened by triangular, wooden joining-blocks. The design could be modified to replace this flat wooden seat with a detachable upholstered seat that fits into the opening between the four seat rails, supported by the insertion of corner blocks, as used in the reproduction Chippendale chair in Chapter 15.

Pine is the chosen material for the dining chair, although it could just as easily be made from oak or ash. It can be kept to the same pale straw colour, or given a bolder, darker look by making it out of afrormosia and treating it with teak oil to bring out a deep brown shine, as of burnished teak. The design has plenty of scope to be adapted in several ways to suit not only personal preference but

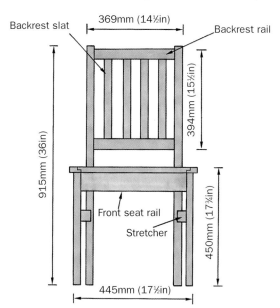

Front elevation.

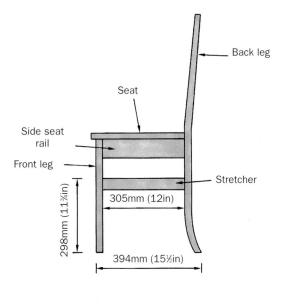

Side elevation.

The finished dining-chair.

The Pine Dining-chair Cutting List

Front leg:	Two of 432 × 32 × 32mm (17 × 1¼ × 1¼in)
Back leg:	Two of 915 × 75 × 50mm (36 × 3 × 2in)
Front seat rail:	One of 420 × 70 × 19mm (16½ × 2¾ × ¾in)
Back seat rail:	One of 343 × 70 × 19mm (13½ × 2¾ × ¾in)
Side seat rail:	Two of 346 × 70 × 19mm (13⅝ × 2¾ × ¾in)
Stretcher:	Two of 346 × 45 × 19mm (13⅝ × 1¾ × ¾in)
Backrest rail:	Two of 343 × 45 × 32mm (13½ × 1¾ × 1¼in)
Backrest slat:	Four of 320 × 32 × 16mm (12⅝ × 1¼ × ⅝in)
Seat panel:	One of 394 × 362 × 19mm (15½ × 14¼ × ¾in)
Seat end-piece:	Two of 346 × 42 × 19mm (13⅝ × 1⅝ × ¾in)

also to match existing furniture or room decoration.

It has been remarked upon previously but the point is worth repeating: if you choose pine, you have to accept that the wood will contain plenty of knots, though some softwoods of the pine variety seem to have more than others. When you purchase the wood, you need to be as selective as possible, avoiding any pieces that have large black dead knots or knots where the centre has already dropped out. Some of the timber that is sold for general carpentry and joinery may not stand close scrutiny for fine work, so you must be prepared to sort through the stock and select the best pieces. As well as looking out for the worst of the knots, you also want to avoid pieces that are badly warped or have the shakes.

The problem is exaggerated if you decide to make a set of chairs to this design, for you increase the amount of wood required, and yet you will want consistency in the supply in order to ensure that all of the chairs look basically the same. It would spoil the collective

look of the chairs if one were to be virtually knot-free, whilst another was covered in them.

As it is very likely that this chair will be one of a set, it is also necessary to make certain that all of the parts can be cut to the same shape and size several times over. For shaped components, such as the back legs and backrest rails, this means making templates. Usually, thick paper or thin card is good enough material for this purpose, unless you are thinking of going into mass production, in which case plywood templates would be better!

Starting with the two back legs, mark and cut out the template so that the bottom 100mm (4in) has a pronounced backward curve, followed by a straight vertical portion that reaches up as high as the level of the seat, after which the upright section is raked back in a straight line, tapering slightly towards the top. The overall length of each back leg is 915mm (36in).

Taking two pieces of 75 × 50mm (3 × 2in) sawn wood, plane these to a thickness of 32mm (1¼in), and lay the template in place on each piece to mark out two identical back legs. Cut on the waste side of the line with the jigsaw, and once all the waste has been removed, lightly plane the curves with the spokeshave, and the long straight sections with the smoothing plane. Place the legs side by side to check that they are identical, trimming

Shaping the back leg with the spokeshave.

*Drawing out the brackrest rail with
a French curve.*

*Trimming the backrest rail to shape with
the spokeshave.*

where necessary with the plane or the spokeshave until they agree at every point.

The two backrest rails are identical, and each has a curved shape to make for a more comfortable sitting position. The curve is not uniform, as in the case of the arc of a circle, but is straight at the centre, with a curve at each end. The thickness of both rails is 19mm (¾in) and they are cut from wood measuring 45 × 32mm (1¾ × 1¼in). Although a template is essential if you are making several chairs, for a single example you can mark in the lines with a French curve and a pencil – a much quicker and simpler method. When marking out the two back rails, remember to allow sufficient wood for the tenons. Cut out each backrest rail with the jigsaw, completing the shaping with the spokeshave.

All of the seat rails are cut from 70 × 19mm (2¾ × ¾in) wood, and the stretchers which run between the front and back legs measure 45 × 19mm (1¾ × ¾in).

Measure and mark in the mortise positions in each of the back legs. Each of the mortises is cut to a width of 13mm (½in). Scribe two parallel lines with the mortise gauge, set centrally across the width of the wood, marking them in the indicated positions along the back legs. All of the mortises are set in 6mm (¼in) at each end, so that they and their tenons are concealed from view, and the depth to which

each mortise is cut should be 19mm (¾in).

Once the mortise has been clearly marked on the surface of the wood, the quickest and easiest way of cutting it is to remove most of the waste with a drill before chopping out the remainder with the chisel and mallet. The pillar drill or vertical drill stand is ideal for the initial boring of the holes, using a 9mm (⅜in) diameter wood drill, especially if this particular tool is fitted with a depth gauge, since this will enable you to drill accurately a series of holes. Note that whereas the mortises for the backrest and stretcher rails are stopped, those for the seat rails meet inside the piece, since each of the legs has two mortises cut in adjacent faces.

It will simplify matters at this stage if you mark and cut the mortises in the two front legs, each of which is prepared from 32 × 32mm (1¼ × 1¼in) material measuring 432mm (17in) long.

Start by making the chairback. The two back legs are parallel with each other, so the two backrest rails and the back seat rail are of exactly the same length – 305mm (12in) minus the tenons. Taking each rail in turn, mark a tenon at either end and cut away the shoulders with the tenon saw. As the mortises are all inset at both ends, each tenon should have secondary shoulders cut to match. Check the fitting of the joints between all three rails and the two back legs: there should be an overall squareness to the assembly, otherwise the chair, when it is finished, will be lopsided.

The gap between the top and bottom backrest rails is filled with four vertical slats cut from 32 × 16mm (1¼ × ⅝in) wood, each spaced at regular intervals, and fitted in place with mortise and tenon joints. Each mortise is 6mm (¼in) wide, marked to a length of 25mm (1in), which allows for a 3mm (⅛in) inset at each end. It is possible to mark in the mortises with the gauge, although the curved shape of the two backrest rails means that the gauged lines will tend to follow the curve rather than running straight, which a mortise should. Therefore you must use these lines as a guide only, and compensate by eye. Cut each mortise to a depth of 6mm (¼in); there is little to be gained in this instance by drilling a series of holes first, since the amount of waste that needs to be removed from each mortise is small.

Measure the distance between the two backrest rails to determine the length of the four slats. They should be 305mm (12in) each minus the tenons, but this figure is based on the assumption that you have followed the measurements in the diagram precisely, something that is very difficult to achieve in reality. It is far safer to treat the quoted measurements as a guide, and to rely only on the lengths indicated by your own tape measure. When you know how long the slats should be, mark them out on to the material, adding the tenons, and cut these to size in the usual way.

Before assembling the chairback, cut a mitre at the end of each tenon in the back seat rail, so that this leaves room to receive similarly mitred tenons when the side seat rails are prepared and fitted.

Apply wood glue to the joints and begin by assembling the four slats between the two backrest rails. Fit this assembly to one back leg, together with the rear seat rail, and place the second back leg in position. Tap the joints fully home with the mallet and a clean block of wood. If any glue squeezes out from the joints, wipe it away with a damp cloth and clamp the

Assembling the backrest.

Assembling the chairback.

chairback assembly whilst the glue dries.

With the completion of the back, the next step is to cut and joint the seat rails and stretchers that join the chairback to the two front legs. The two front legs having already had their mortises cut, it only remains to measure and cut the rails to length and mark the tenons at each end. However, the tenons in the side seat rails and the stretchers cannot be cut normally, because the width of the chair at the back is 372mm (14⅝in) compared with a width of 448mm (17⅝in) at the front, so the side rails and stretchers will need to be set at an angle, and this means that the tenons at the end of each rail cannot run parallel with the rail, as would usually be the case, but must be marked and cut at the required angle.

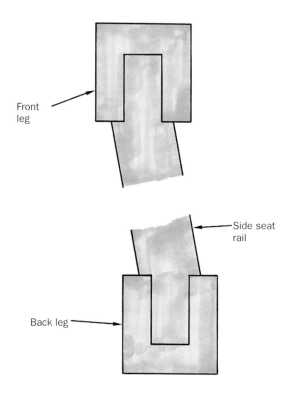

Front
leg

Side seat
rail

Back leg

Plan of front leg, back leg and rail,
showing the angling of the tenons.

Assembling the chair frame.

Start by joining the front seat rail to the two front legs. This is perfectly straightforward, because the tenons are cut conventionally, except that they need a mitre to be cut at their ends. Glue the joints together, checking that they are square.

A template should now be made for the side seat rails, to provide an accurate pattern for the tenon angles. One way of preparing the template is to take a large sheet of paper and draw a full-sized plan of the chair. Each side seat rail, which measures 305mm (12in) long minus the tenons, is then marked up with its tenons, complete with their correct angles, noting that the tenon that fits into the back leg is angled outwards, and the tenon that fits into the front leg is angled inwards. Repeat the same marking out process for the two stretchers. Cut the tenons in the usual way, mitring the ends of

the side seat rails so that they butt up against the ends of the tenons in the front and back seat rails, already fitted to the legs. Make a test-fit of the chair to check that the overall structure is correct and stands properly on a flat surface. When you are satisfied that all is well, glue the remaining joints together and cramp up the assembly until the glue has dried thoroughly.

The seat is made from solid wood and takes the form of three tongued-and grooved boards joined together, with four V-shaped grooves cut along the direction of the grain, and two wedge-shaped pieces of wood used to cover the end-grain and to add a finishing touch. The seat is made in the shape of a trapezium, to match the layout of the seat rails, and it is notched on its two back corners to fit around the back legs.

Assembling the tongued-and-grooved boards for the seat.

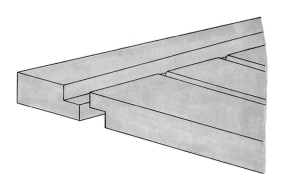

Exploded halved joint between main part of seat and end-piece.

Cutting V-grooves with the electric router.

The seat components ready for assembly.

Start by cutting the tongued-and-grooved boards longer than required, and glue them together into a single panel. As each individual board measures 146 × 19mm (5¾ × ¾in), including the tongue, when the three boards are assembled, the width will be 425mm (16¾in), whereas the seat panel should only be 362mm (14¼in) wide. Trim 6mm (¼in) from the rear edge by planing away the groove and cut a further 58mm (2¼in) from the front edge, including the tongue. The four V-shaped grooves are made with the electric router fitted with an appropriate V-cutter; two of the grooves following the joint line between the boards, the other two being placed in such a way that each groove seems to be separated by an equal distance, except for the first segment, which is wider than the others.

Mark up the panel so that it measures 327mm (12⅞in) in length at the back of the seat, and 394mm (15½in) at the front. Cut off the waste from the ends with the jigsaw. Now measure and mark the position of the two notches, which allow the seat to fit around the back legs, bringing its rear edge to within 6mm (¼in) of the rear face of the back seat rail, the front edge of the seat jutting 6mm (¼in) beyond the front legs.

The two wedge-shaped end-pieces measure 343mm (13½in) in length, and each is 22mm (⅞in) wide at the back and 32mm (1¼in) wide at the front. In addition, a further 6mm (¼in) should be allowed with the width to take into account the halved joint overlap. Since both

Three-sided wooden joining block fastening underside of seat to inside of seat rail.

halves of the joint are cut as rebates, you may find it easier to rebate the wood used to make the end-pieces before it is cut to size. The best tool for this task is the electric router fitted with a rebate cutter, set to a precise depth of 9.5mm (⅜in). Rebate the underside of the main seat panel likewise, and fit both parts together to check that the rebates correspond perfectly. Glue the two end-pieces in position, and when this has dried completely, rub down the seat thoroughly with sandpaper and fit it into place on the four seat rails. When you are satisfied that the seat and the frame of the chair are in correct alignment, apply glue to the abutting surfaces to create an initial bond, and then reinforce this by gluing triangular wooden joining blocks between the inside surfaces of the seat rails and the underside of the seat.

With only small modifications, an upholstered drop-in seat could be made instead of the solid seat. The method is described in the following chapter.

The type of finish that you apply to the chair depends on the choice of wood and the effect you wish to achieve. The illustrated example is a pine chair, so it was stained a light oak colour, which would be equally suitable for a chair made of ash or oak. There are other possibilities: afrormosia will produce the appearance of teak, and utile or sapele are both a good basis for the colour of mahogany. The same chair can be given many different finishes.

CHAPTER 15

The Reproduction Chippendale Chair

In an age when elegance is still appreciated but can be increasingly hard to find, this reproduction version of a chair design, which dates from the late 1770s, is a delight to behold, and we must be thankful that it existed in the first place, giving us something that is so worthwhile and satisfying to copy.

This particular design, at first glance, has a somewhat ordinary, conventional appearance but, on closer examination, it is its very simplicity that gives it such appeal. Thomas Chippendale would have made it in mahogany; the back legs are curved and taper as they diverge upwards; but it is the backrest splat that holds the attention, with its graceful lines, in the inverted vase shape that was so frequently used. There is reeding on the top edge of the front and side seat rails, and the upholstered seat is set within the rails, supported on corner blocks. An original example has the advantage

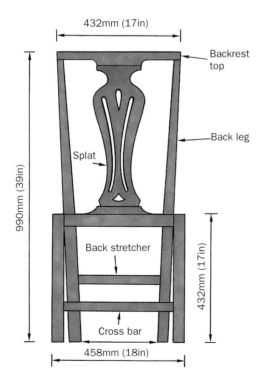

Front elevation.

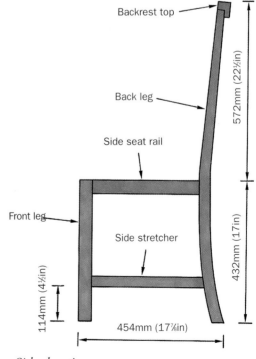

Side elevation.

The finished Chippendale chair.

with a 6mm (¼in) chisel. The narrow blade width is preferred in this instance because it cuts well with the minimum of pressure.

The corresponding tenons may be marked in with the mortise gauge, since the uprights still have squared surfaces. Cut away the main shoulders with the tenon saw, measuring the second pair of shoulders to match precisely the mortise. Trim the tenon and make a trial fitting of the joint.

Fit the stretcher rail that joins the two back

Sandpapering the backrest.

legs. This is cut from 32 × 19mm (1¼ × ¾in) material and is set 228mm (9in) up from the bottom of the legs, where it is arranged to lie flush with the rear edge. In this case, the tenons are almost bare-faced, with only a very shallow shoulder on one side to make sure that the mortise is concealed from view, and this, indeed, sets the pattern for all the remaining mortise and tenon joints used to fit the front and side seat rails, and the stretchers between front and back legs. Each is 9mm (⅜in) wide and is placed 9mm (⅜in) from the outside edge. In the case of the seat rails, the mortises are 32mm (1¼in) long and the stretcher mortises are 25mm (1in) long. Remember that the back stretcher rail will have angled tenon shoulders, as with the rear seat rail, to take into account the convergence of the back legs.

This is a good opportunity to mark and cut all of the mortises, including those in the two front legs. The stretcher rails between the front and back legs are set 150mm (6in) up from the bottom end. The seat rail mortises are cut to a depth of 19mm (¾in), whereas the stretcher rail mortises are 13mm (½in) deep.

The next step is to make the splat for the

Trial-fitting of the backrest to the uprights of the back legs.

119

back of the chair. A template has already been prepared for this, so transfer the pattern on to a piece of wood. The finished splat measures 13mm (½in) thick, so you can either copy the template directly on to a piece of sapele, which is already planed to this thickness, or mark it out on to a piece of rough-sawn material and plane it down yourself. In either case, the outline of the splat, together with its cutaways, need to be clearly marked and cut to size with the jigsaw.

For the four cut-out portions, drill a hole through each one to admit the blade of the jigsaw. File and sandpaper all of the sawn edges until they are perfectly smooth.

The splat is fitted to the backrest with a simple housing joint, and its bottom end slots into a groove cut in the top edge of the back seat rail. This is straightforward jointing and the only real complication concerns the fact that the backrest is curved and the splat is straight, but this is resolved at the outset, before any jointing is attempted, by lining the splat up beneath the backrest and marking in the shallow curve on the top end of the splat. You will see that only a small amount of shaping is needed to produce a concave surface at the top

of the splat, which matches precisely the curvature of the backrest. Measure and mark in the position of the housing joint groove in the underside of the backrest, and cut this to size with the 6mm (¼in) chisel, and then prepare a matching bare-faced tongue at the top of the splat, the depth being no more than 9mm (⅜in).

The groove in the back seat rail should be 13mm (½in) wide, to receive the full thickness of the splat, and measures 136mm (5⅜in) long and 9mm (⅜in) deep.

When all the pieces are completed satisfactorily, and the joints all fit together perfectly, make a trial assembly of the chairback, consisting of the two back legs, the rear seat rail, the rear stretcher, backrest and splat. Once you are satisfied that all of the joints are sound, this is the best moment to mark the amount of trimming required at the top of each upright to bring it into alignment with the curve of the backrest. Mark the amount that needs to be cut away on the end-grain of each upright, then dismantle the components and plane the front edge of both uprights with the spokeshave. Also, if you originally cut the backrest slightly too long, as a safety precaution for the chopping out of the

Cutting out the splat with the jigsaw.